# 700 ASL SENTENCES

# BY

# Don Cabbage, Ph.D.

DON CABBAGE
— PUBLISHING —

ISBN: 978-1-966954-56-9 (paperback)
ISBN: 978-1-966954-57-6 (hardcover)
ISBN: 978-1-966954-58-3 (epub)

Library of Congress Control Number: 2025913397

Lets get started:

Learning sign language is an adventure into a new world of communication. All of our linguistic learning to be connected to our auditory sensors. Sign language however has nothing to do with our auditory sensors. It is "Gestural Communication". All concepts are related to movement of the hand. Those movements represent pictures, symbols, or abstract concepts. One movement of the hands cam represent several possible words in spoken language. To speak in gestural language one must learn to think in pictures or physical symbols ti represent concepts. Gestural communication is an amazing form of communication that varies in each country's language. The root of sign language is set in the respective indigenous culture of each country. In some countries with similar cultures symbols may be the same or similar to those in other countries. In other countries the symbols are strictly akin to the culture of that specific country. Now lets get started and remember every time you move your hand it means something. Enjoy learning to express yourself even more with your hands.

Donald T. Cabbage, Ph.D.
PO Box 371997
El Paso, TX 79937
915 330-4887
dc@missionsociety.us

Objective: Interested in Teaching classes in ASL multi-levels. Professional interpreting in various sign languages.

Education:
PhD, Educational Admin: Louisiana Baptist University, Shreveport, LA
PhD, Education of the Hearing Impaired: Freedom University, Orlando, FL
Master Christian Education: Freedom University, Orlando
Bachelor of Science: Tennessee Temple University, Chattanooga, TN

Experience:
2008 -2015 have been establishing English language Christian Schools in the Republic of Korea and consulting deaf ministries in China. 30 Christian schools we have helped to establish along with the Korean Association of Christian Schools.

2008-2015 taught Bible lessons on the Far East Broadcasting Company airways from Seoul, Korea once per week during the English broadcasting segment.

2013 invited by China's government to build an American Tourist town in China including English language schools and Churches. 1967 developed modular American Sign Language Course for establishing deaf ministries in Churches across the USA. That class was used to pioneer the establishing of deaf ministries in hundreds of churches across America. *Among the classes was The Thomas Road Church of Dr. Jerry Falwell of Lynchburg, VA where we put the first sign language interpreters on their now famous Sunday television program.*

From 1967 until 2008 taught sign language and wrote teaching materials in 16 Country sign languages to establish deaf ministries in countries of Canada, Latin America, Caribbean Islands, Micronesia, and island countries of the South Pacific.

1971 assisted in the National Census of the Deaf population serving on the committee to develop question for that census. As member of that committee was invited to the white house for tea with he first lady as thanks for that work.

Assisted Sears Co with the first marketing for the first closed captioning device by writing a survey letter for them to contact the deaf community. 1966 to 1982 working with Bill Rice Ranch Inc. in Murfreesboro, Tennessee responsible for the deaf work and marketing of that ministry saw the summer camp program with deaf people grow from 100 to over 1,500 deaf people for a two week camp.
responsible for bringing 2,000 kids to camp two weeks out of the summer a pioneered the deaf ministries in churches around the country. valuable deaf contacts in virtually every major city in the country.

Have served for 30 years as Certified Sign Language interpreter with contracts that include a Lionbridge Technologies Lionbridge Technologies partnership and SOSi interpreting for the US Department of Homeland Security's Immigration Court and Asylum proceedings. (ASL, LSM, Honduras SL, NSS) Established World Mission Society in 1982 and American Society for the Deaf in 1992.

Author International Sign Language series including ASL, Mexican Sign Language, Brazil Sign Language and others.

Misc: Private pilot with 1,000 hours in the air. Experienced wilderness outdoors man assisted in establishing wilderness camp in Apache Creek, NM in 1975. Written over 20 books. Weekly Radio program on the Far East Broadcasting Company in Seoul Korea 2009 to 2015.

# Introduction

With fifty years of experience and fluency in thirteen different sign languages, Don Cabbage, Ph.D. is an expert in writing and teaching sign. For those wishing to learn the basics of American Sign Language, they now can with Dr. Cabbage's English 700 ASL Sentences. Follow along as beginners will learn the basics of the alphabet and numbers before venturing on to full sentences. After the 700 exercises found in this book, beginners will have a better understanding of this incredible language and have the ability to carry on simple conversations with others.

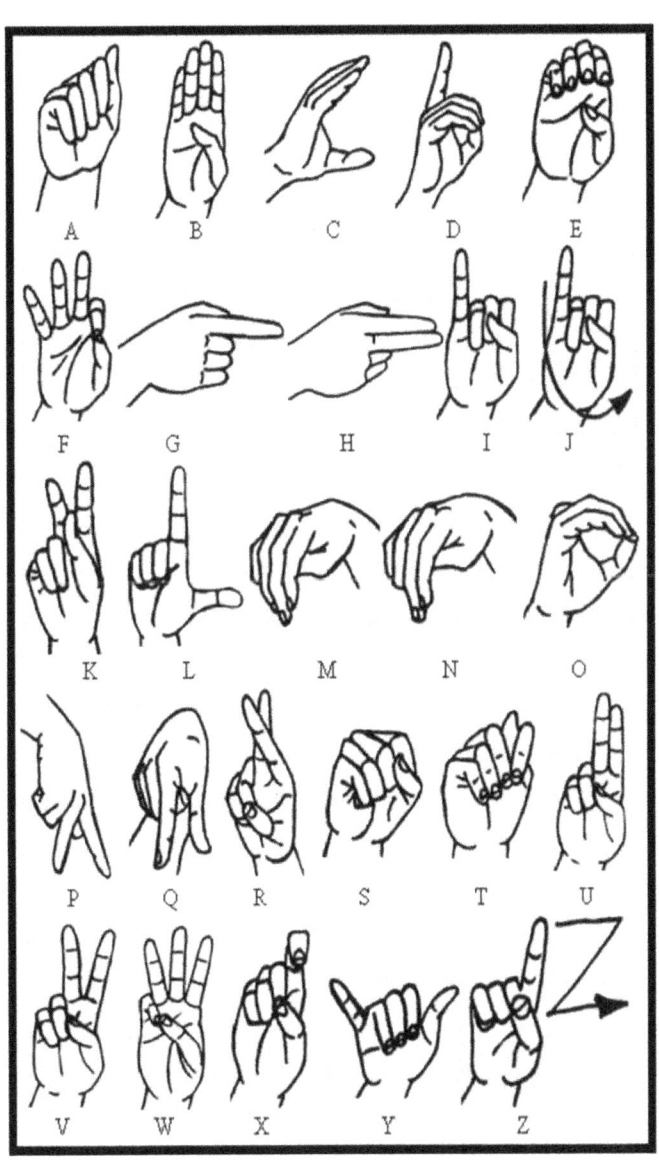

1

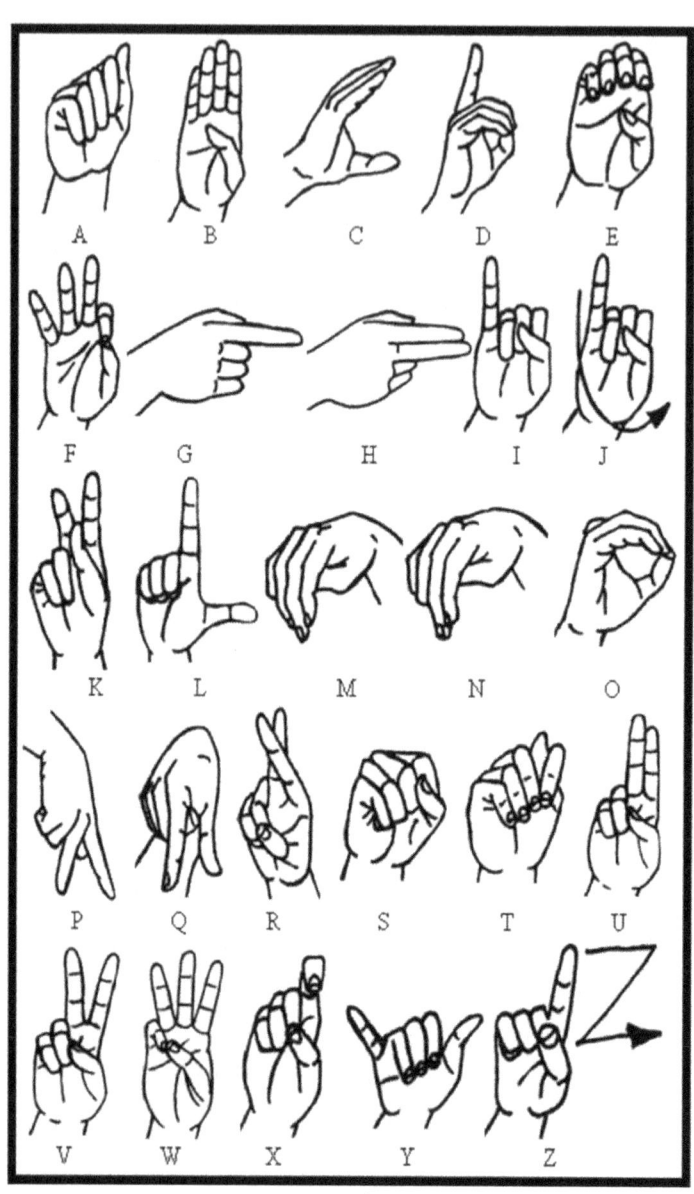

# ASL Numbers

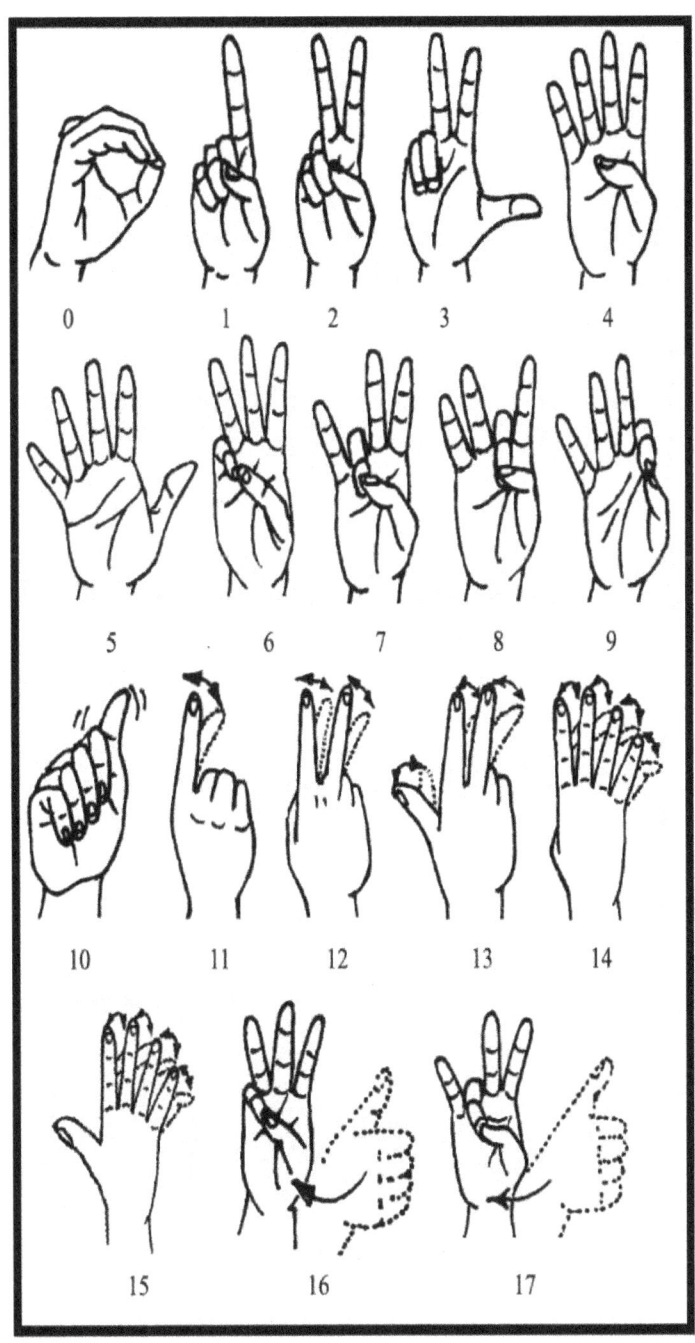

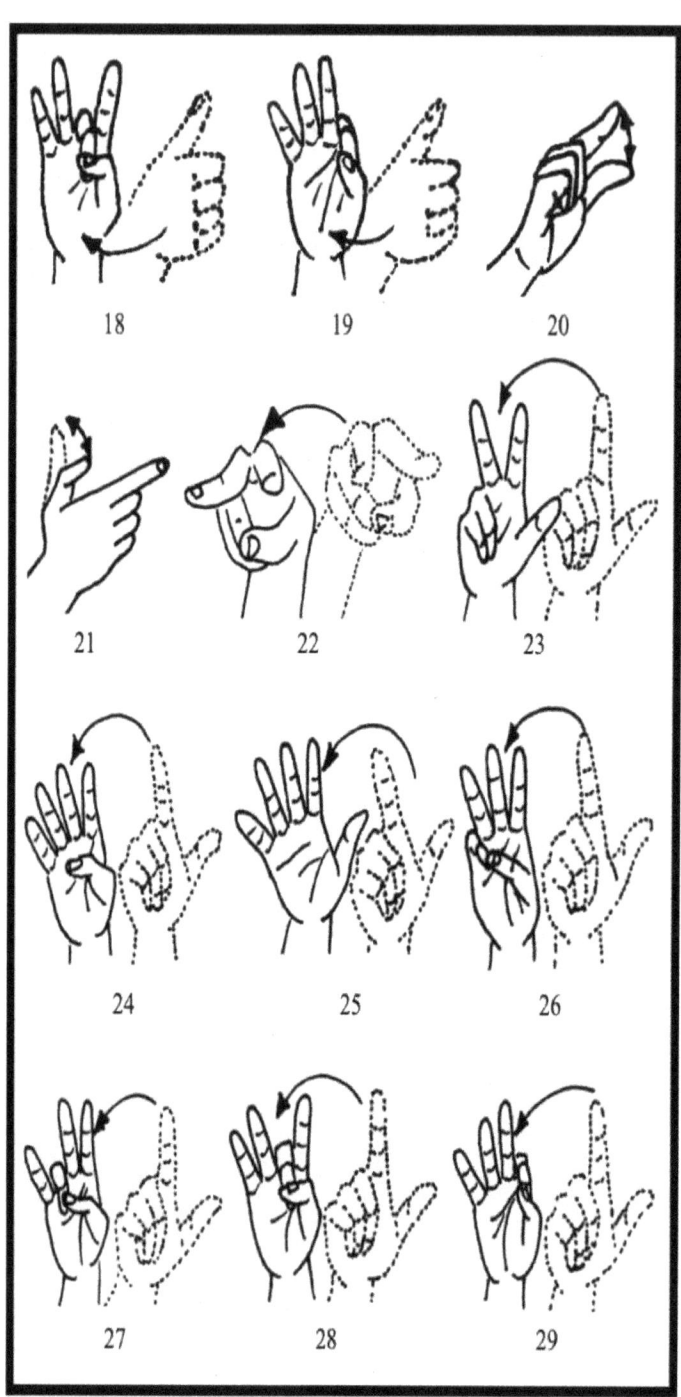

18

19

20

21

22

23

24

25

26

27

28

29

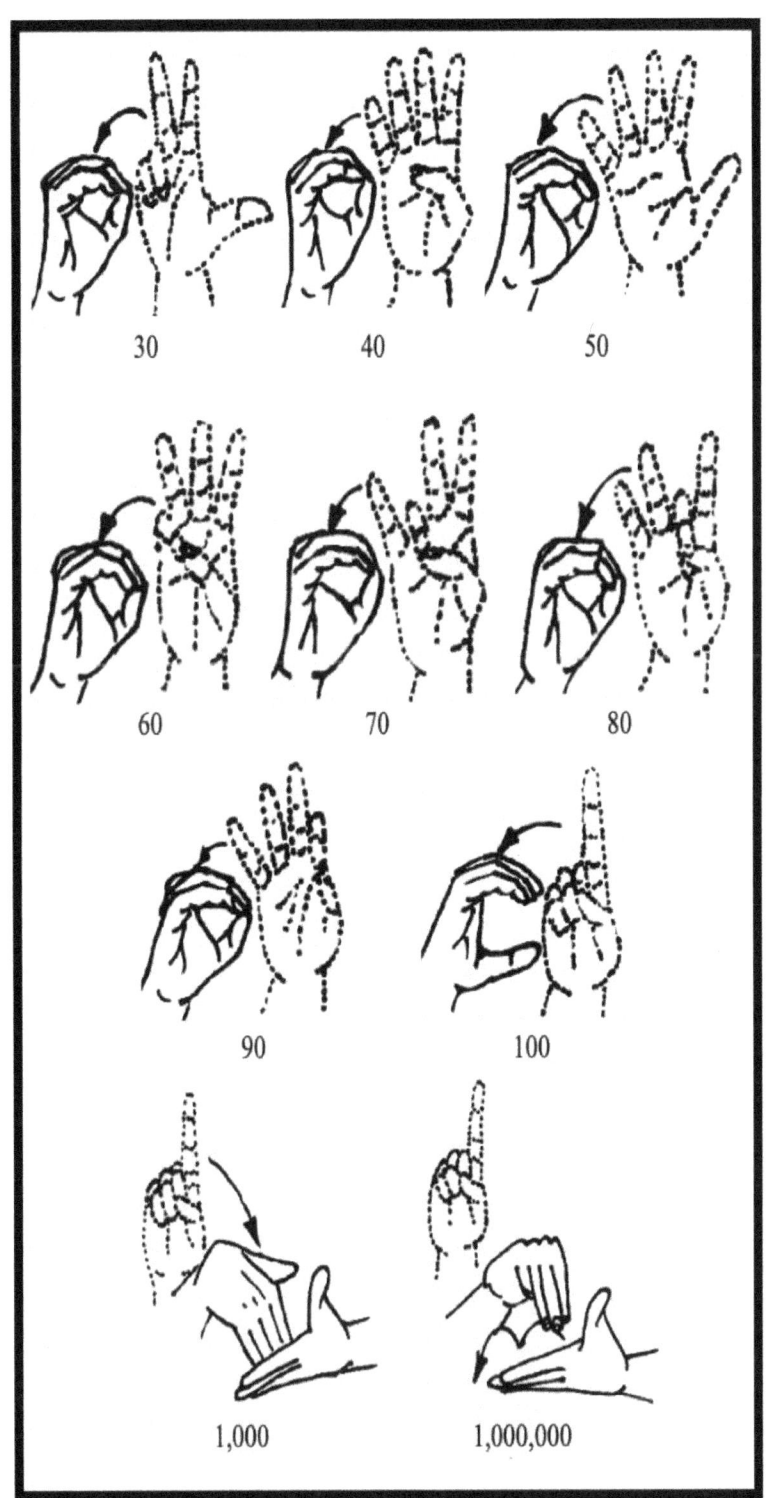

30          40          50

60          70          80

90          100

1,000          1,000,000

#1.　　　Hello.

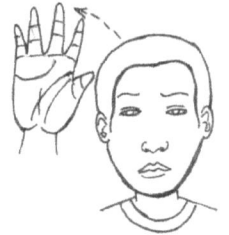

#2

Good　　　morning.

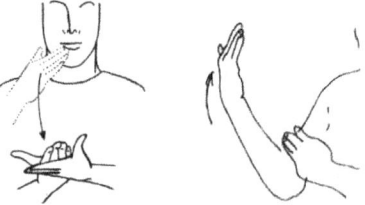

#3

I　　　　am　　　　　John

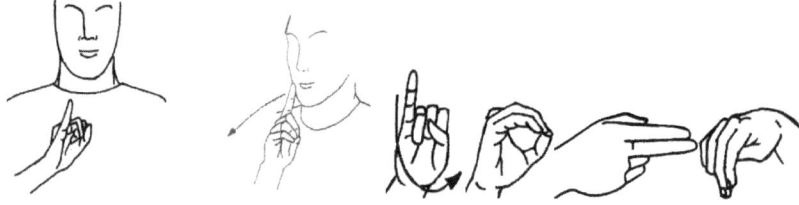

Smith.

#4.

Are    you        Bill            Jones            ?

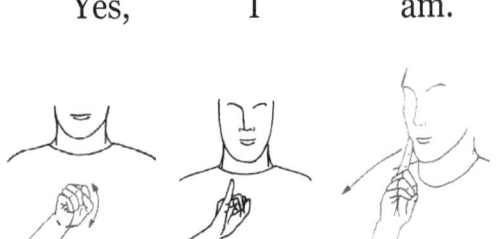

#5.

Yes,        I        am.

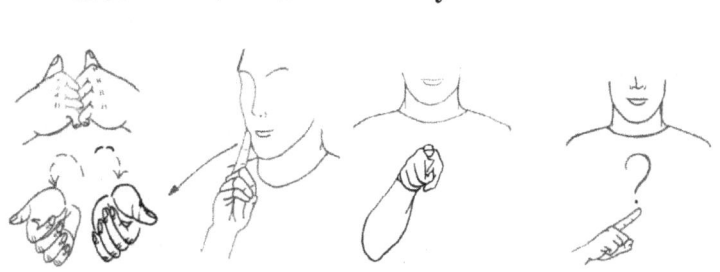

#6.

How            are        you.            ?

#7.

Fine,        thanks.

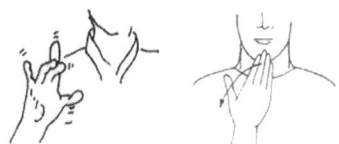


#8.

How        is                          Helen              ?

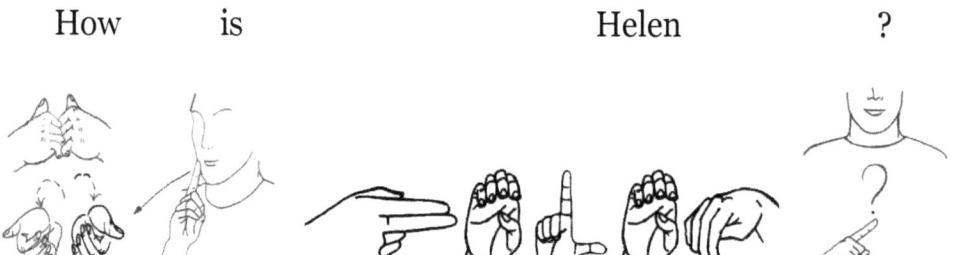


#9.

She        is        very        well,        thank        you.

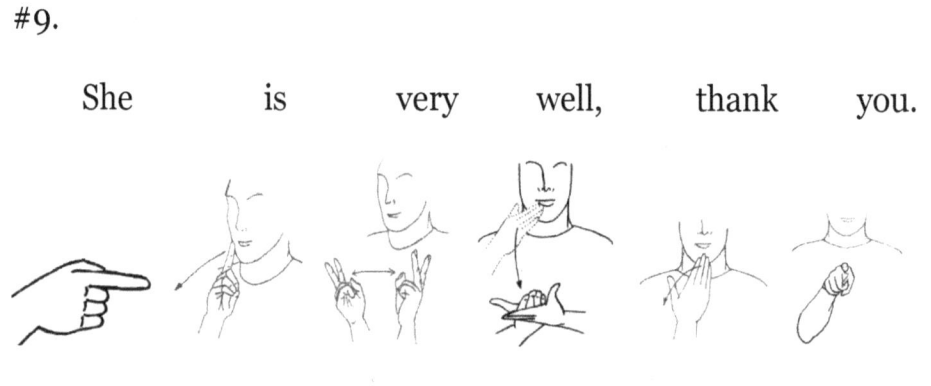

#10.

Good     afternoon,   Mr.           Green.

#11.

Good         evening,      Mrs.          Brown.

#12.

How       are    you      this     evening.  ?

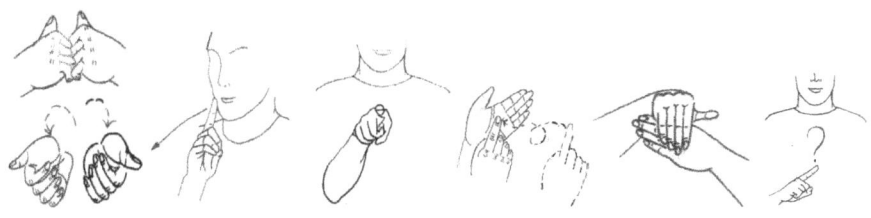

#13.

Good         night,         John.

#14

Good-bye,         Bill.

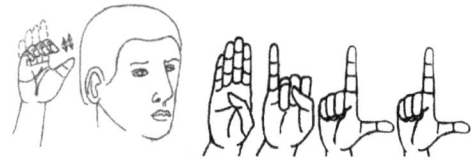

#15

See    you       tomorrow.

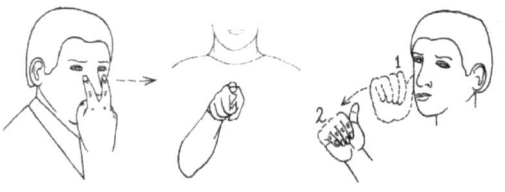

#16.

Come        in,      please.

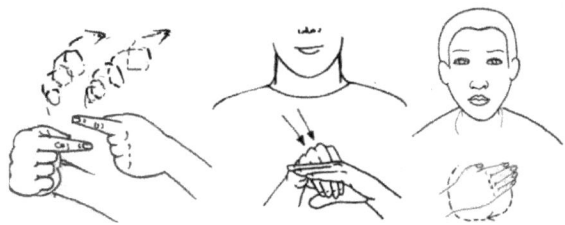

#17.

Sit down.

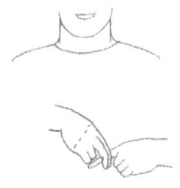

#18.

Stand up,    please.

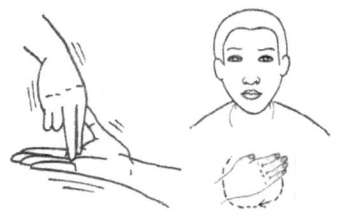

#19

| Open | your | | book, | please. |

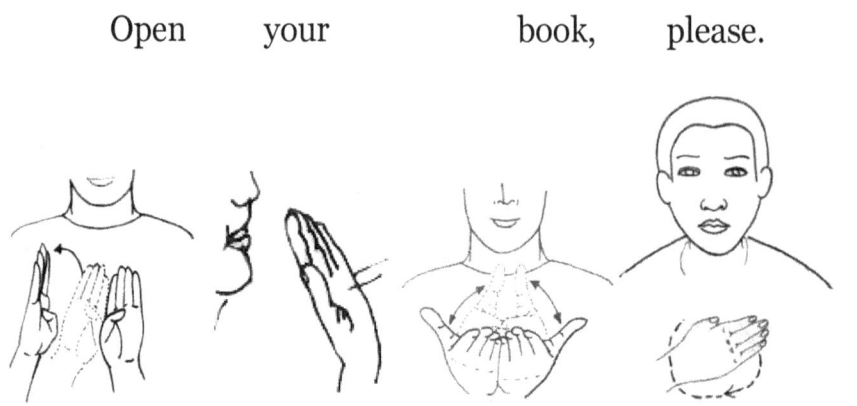

#20

| Close | your | book, | please. |

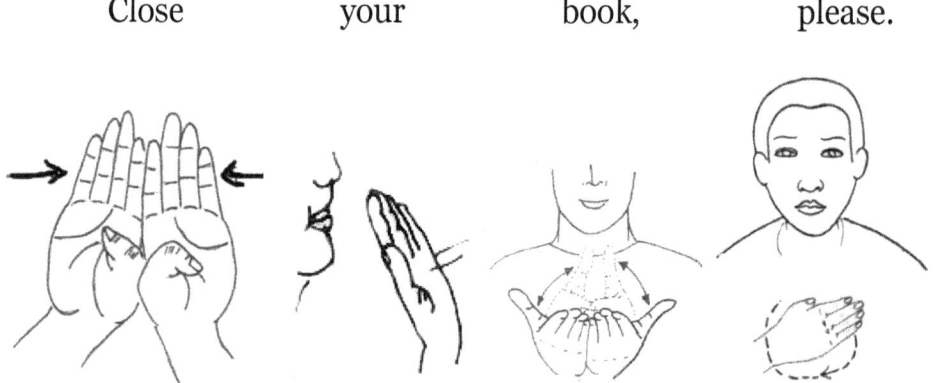

#21

| Don't | open | your | book. |
|---|---|---|---|

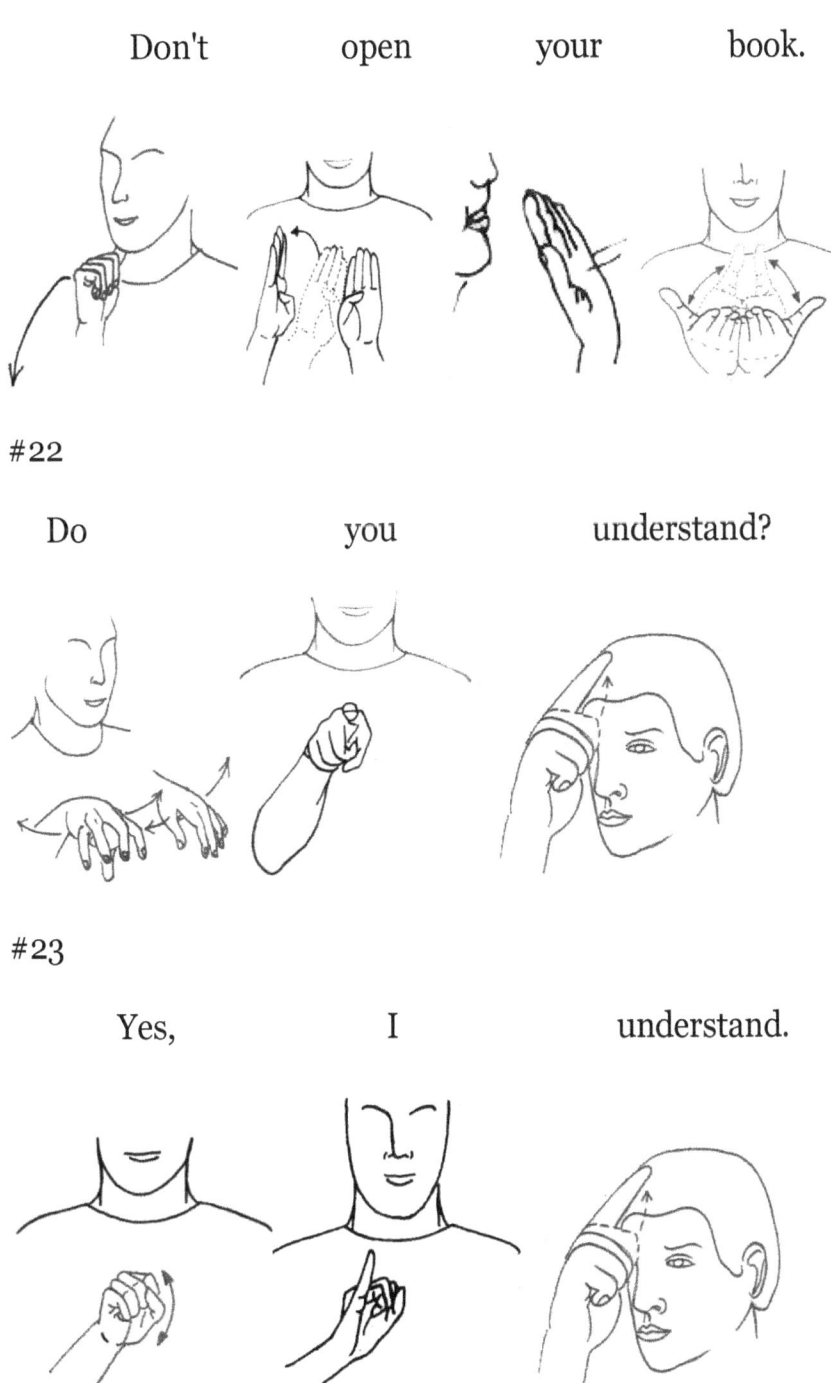

#22

| Do | you | understand? |
|---|---|---|

#23

| Yes, | I | understand. |
|---|---|---|

#24.

| No, | I | do not | understand. |
|---|---|---|---|

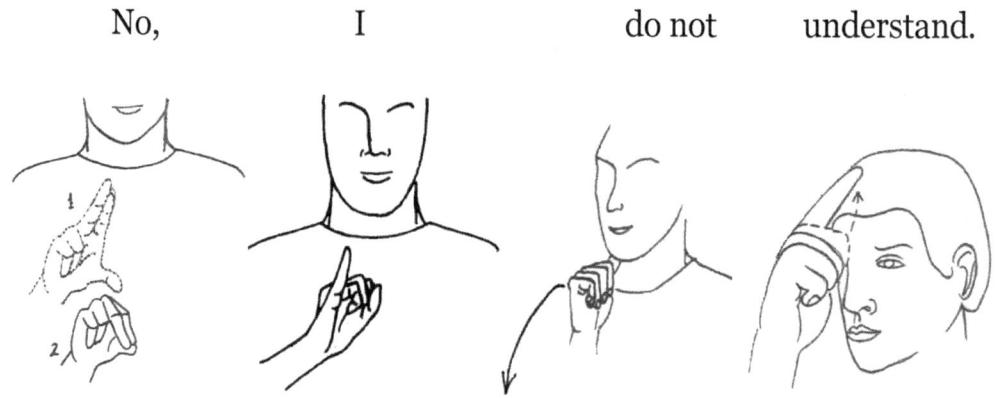

#25

| Listen | and | repeat. |
|---|---|---|

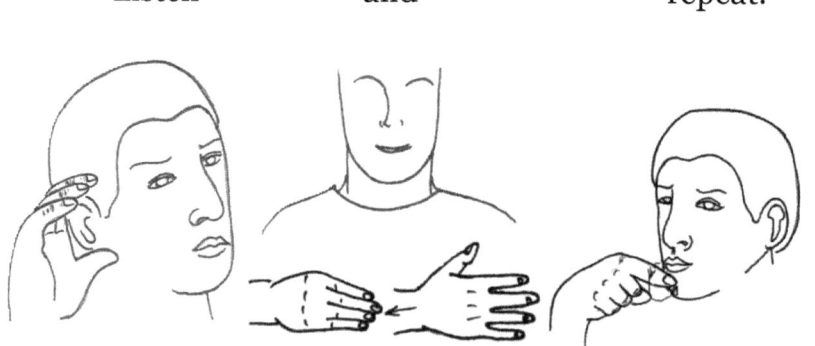

#26

Now          read,          please.

#27

That          is          fine.

#28

It     is     time     to     begin.

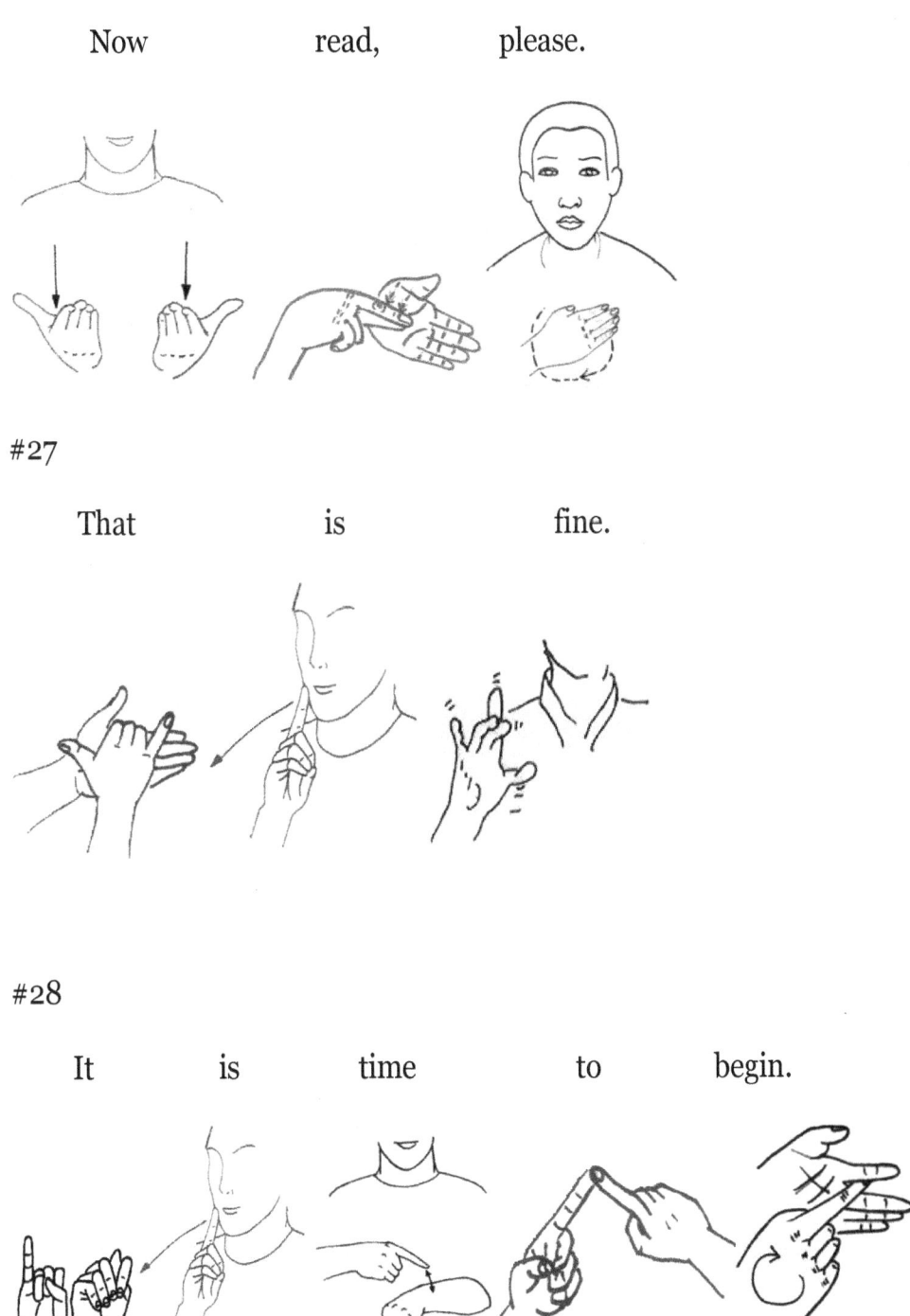

#29

Let us begin now.

#30

This is lesson one.

#31

What is this ?

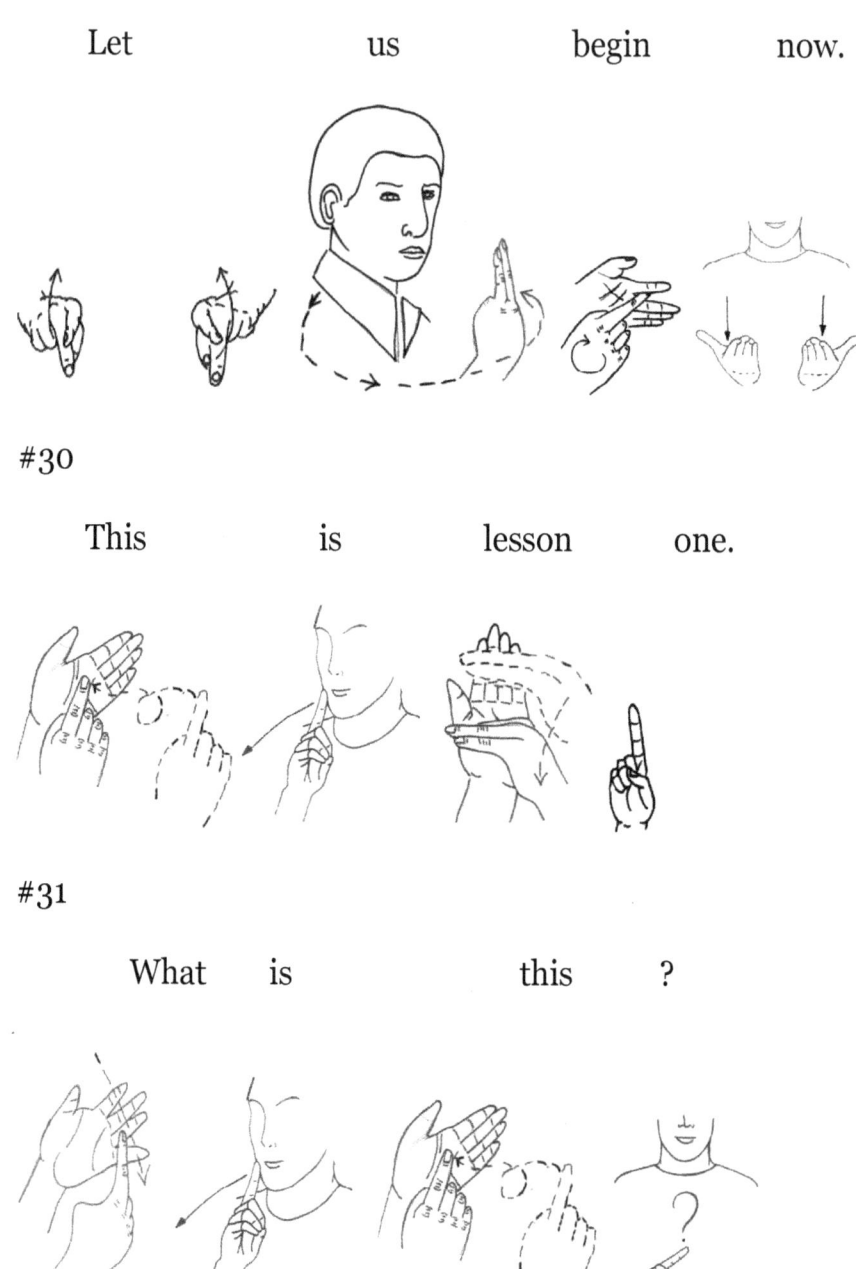

#32

That      is        a        book.

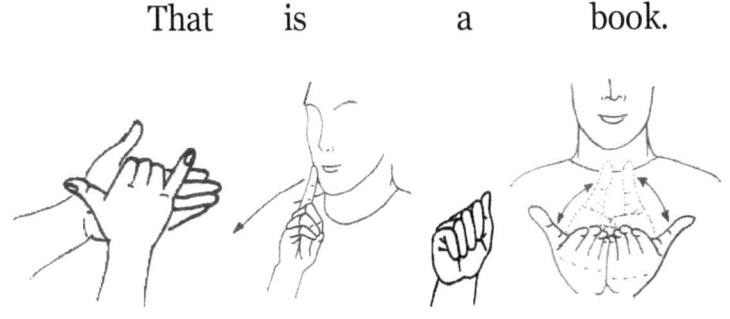

#33

Is        this        your        book    ?

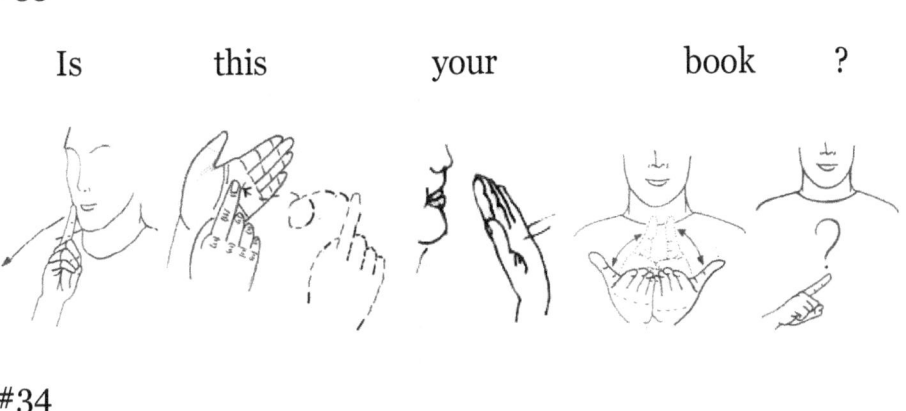

#34

No,     that     is     not     my     book.

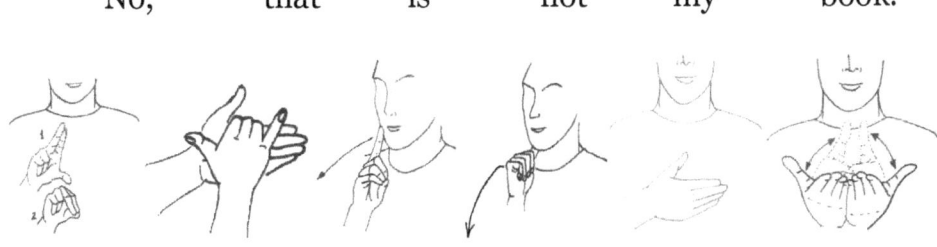

#35

Whose　　　book　　　is　　　　this　　　?

#36

That　　　　is　　　your　　　book.

#37

| And | what | is | that | ? |
|-----|------|-----|------|---|

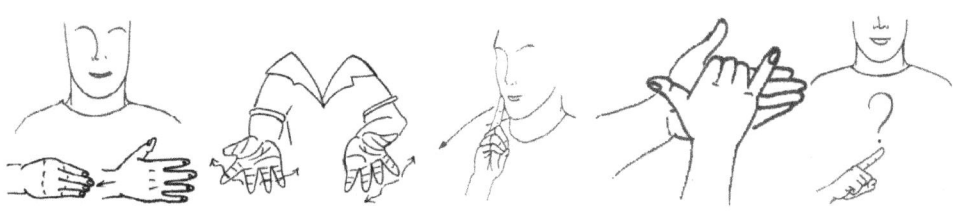

#38

| Is | that | a | book | ? |
|----|------|---|------|---|

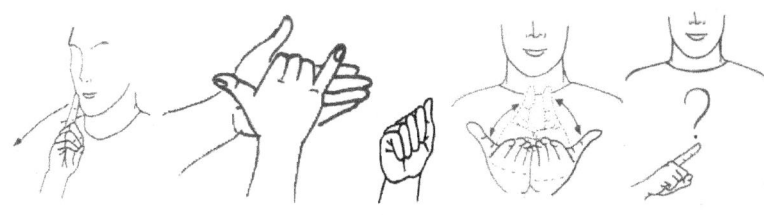

#39

| No, | it | is not. |
|-----|-----|---------|

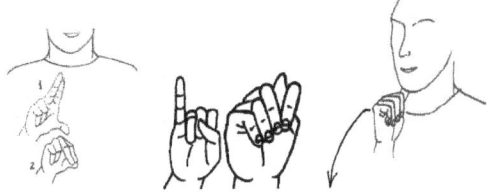

#40

It     is     a     pencil.

#41

Is    it     yours     ?

#42

Yes,    it.    is    mine.

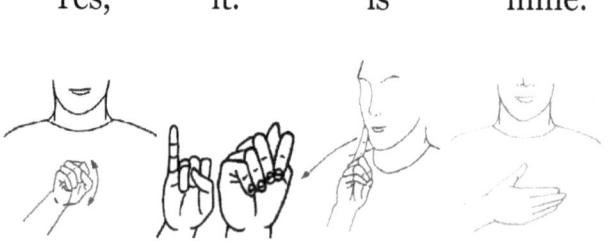

#43

Where     is          the     door          ?

#44

There      it          is.

#45

Is          this          book          his          ?

#46

What     are          these     ?

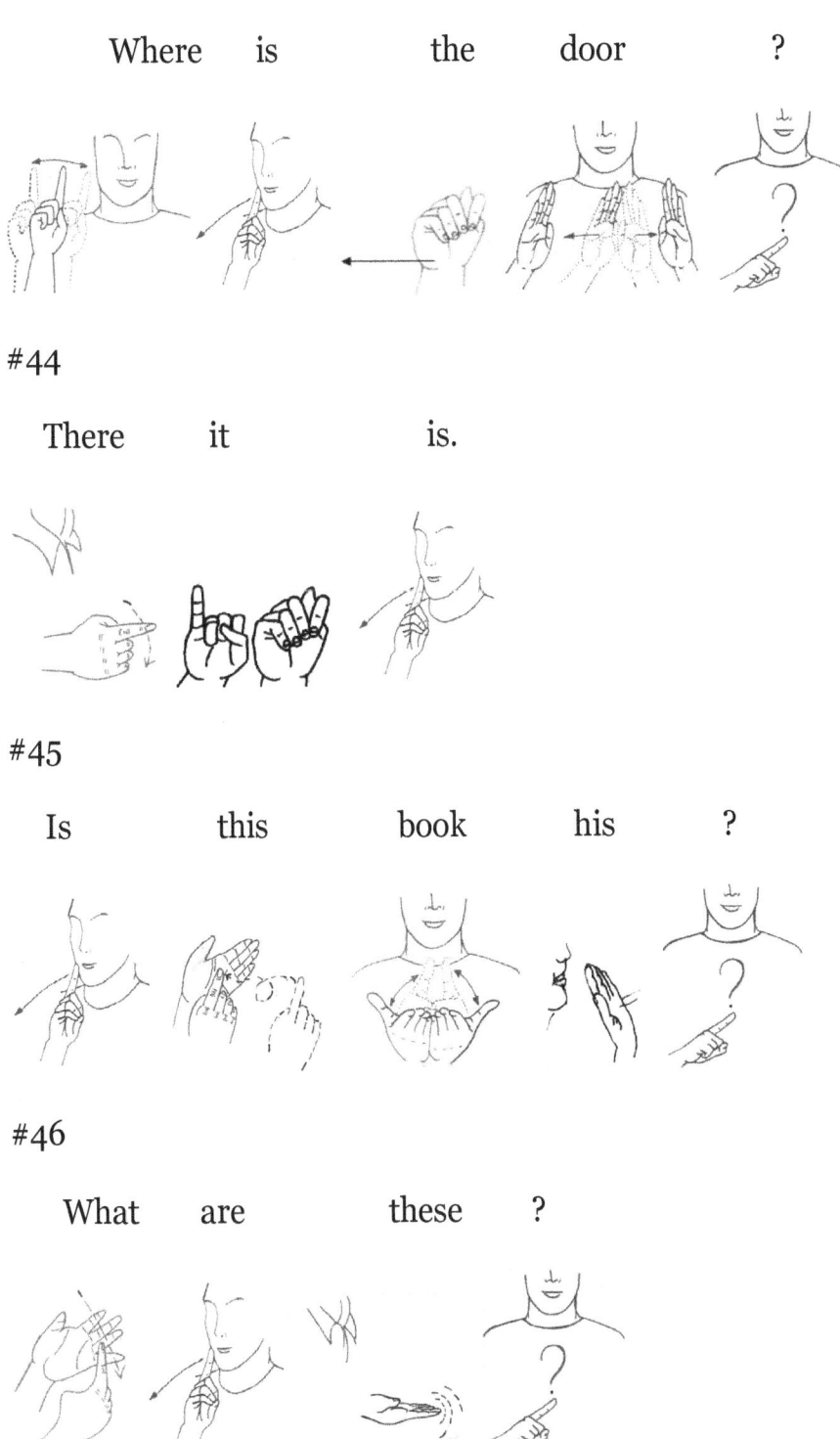

21

#47

Those     are          books.

#48.

Where     are     the     books     ?

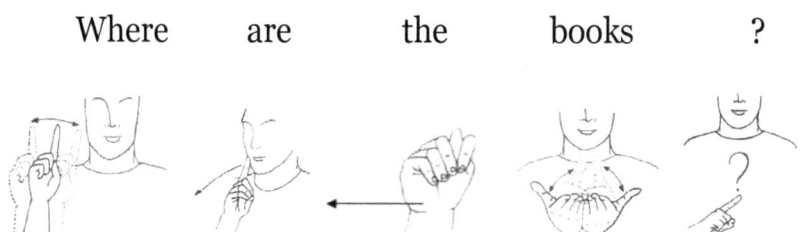

#49.

There    they       are.

#50.

These          are          my          pencils.

#51.

Where      are      your      pens    ?

#52.

They        are        over     there.

#53.

Are     these      your      pens    ?

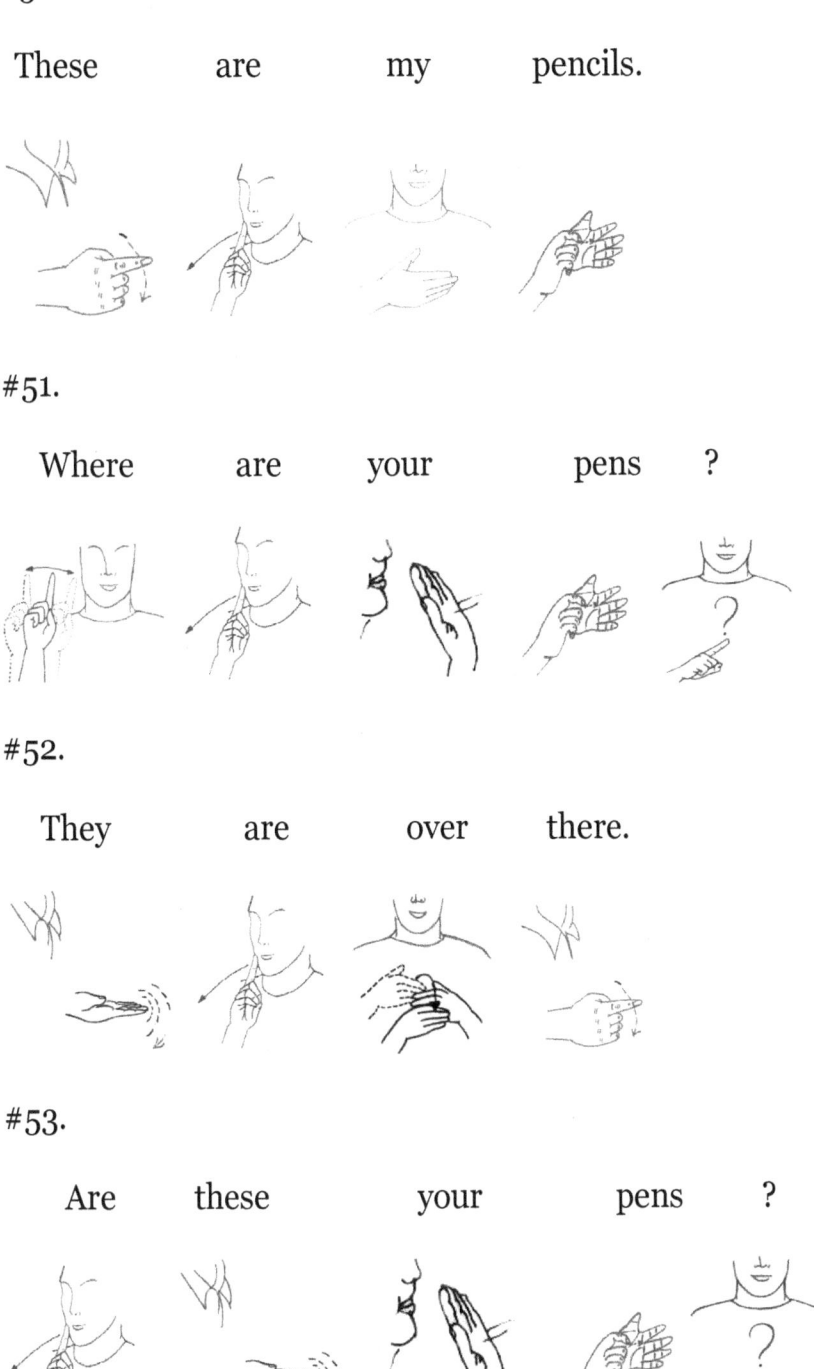

#54.

Yes,        they            are.

#55.

Those            are       mine.

#56.

These             are   your      books,   aren't they  ?

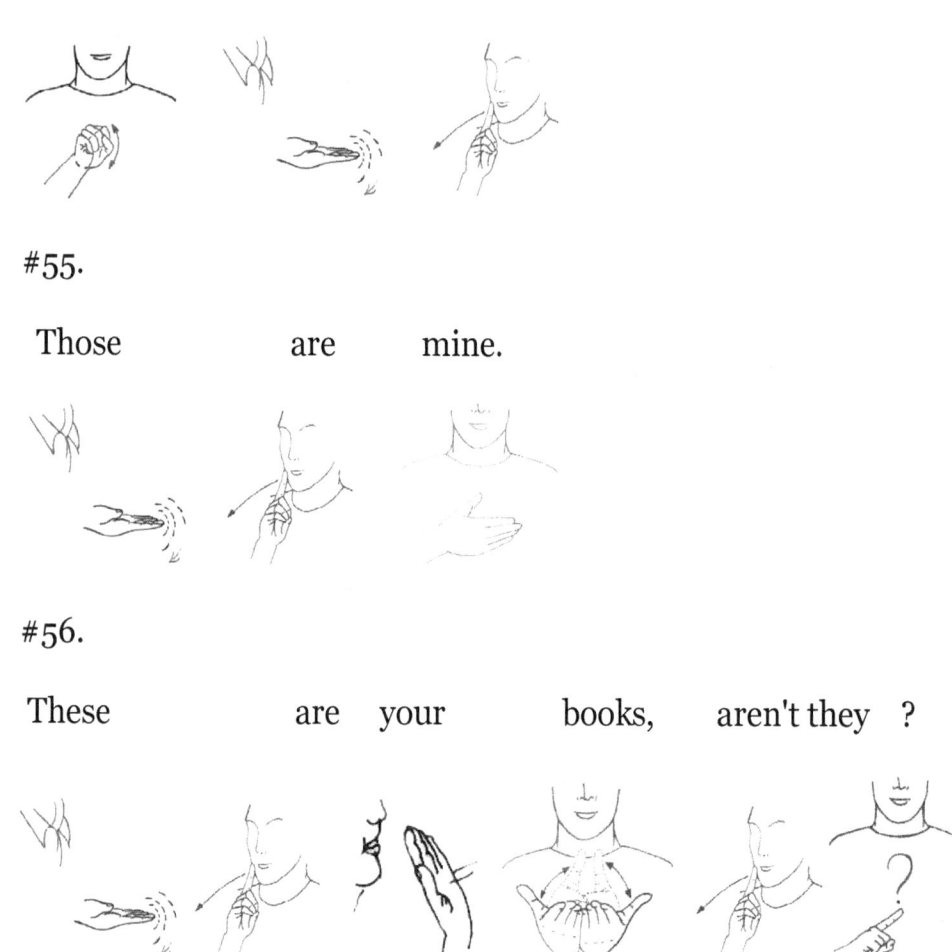

#57.

No,         they         aren't.

#58.

They're         not      mine.

#59.

These        are     mine,    and

those        are     yours.

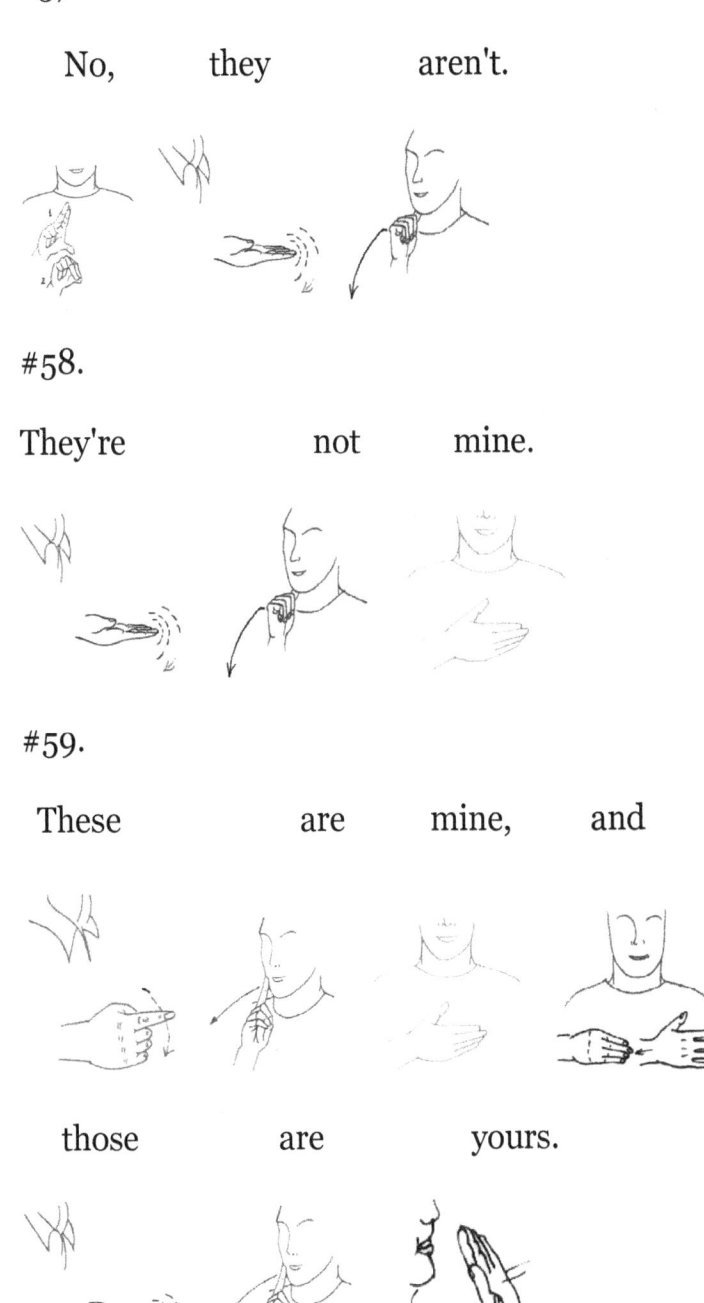

25

#60.

Those        aren't   your      pens,       are they    ?

#61.

Who       are       you       ?

#62.

I      am       a      student.

#63.

Who.       is    that     over there   ?

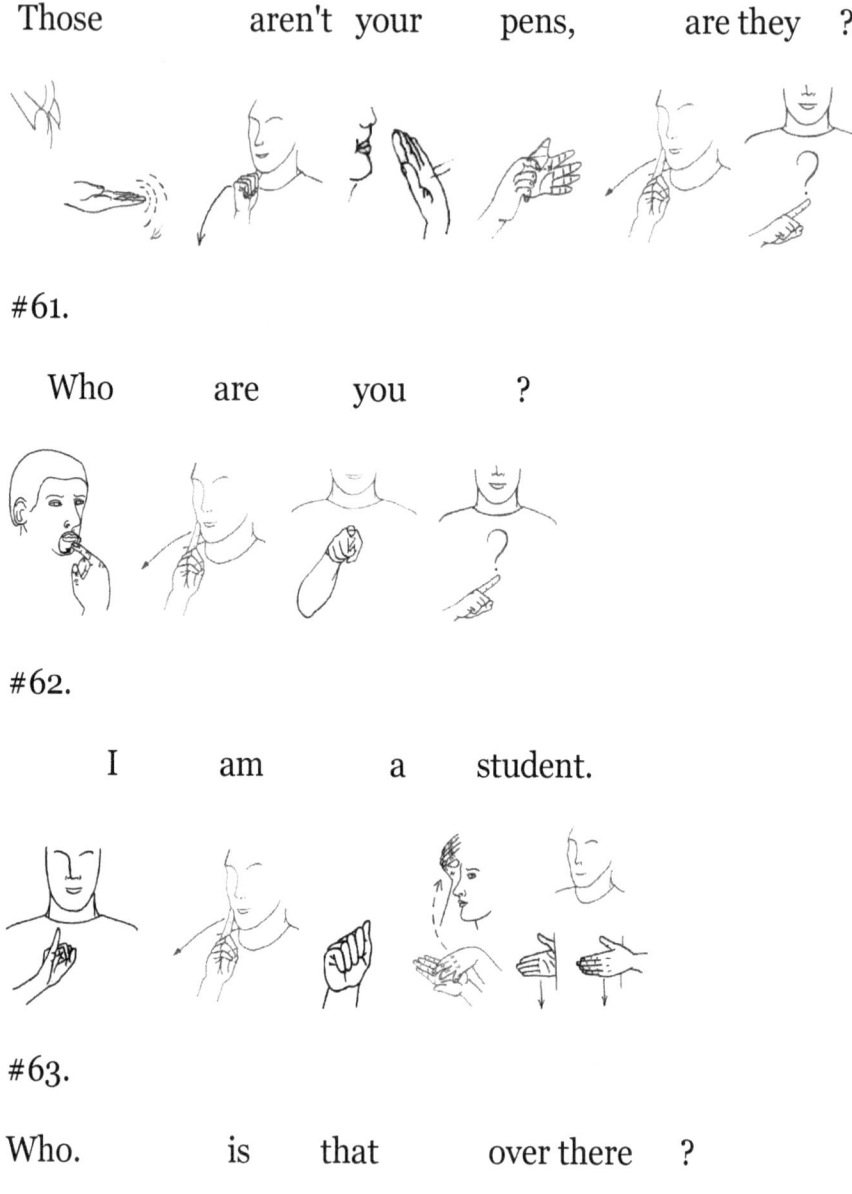

#64.

He          is     a     student,     too.

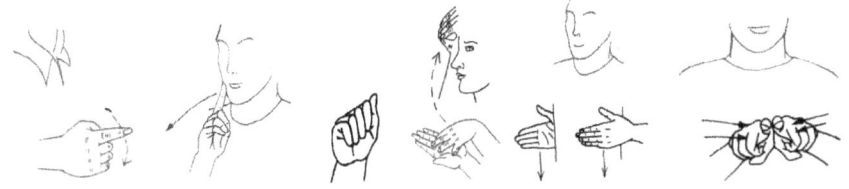

#65.

Is     that  lady  a    student     ?

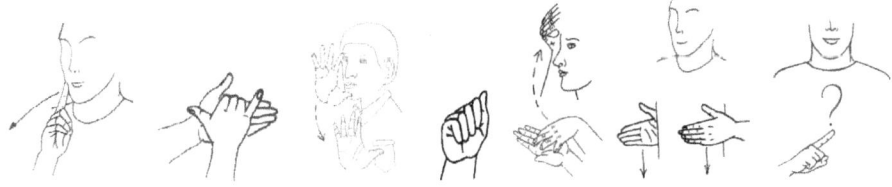

#66.

No,     she   isn't.

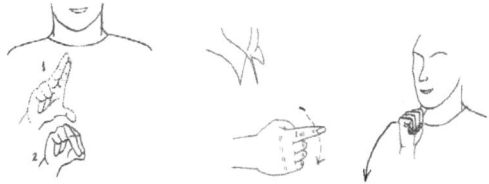

#67

Those    men     aren't  students,   either.

#68.

Am      I      your           teacher      ?

#69.

Yes,      you        are.

#70.

That       man      is      a      teacher,

isn't he    ?

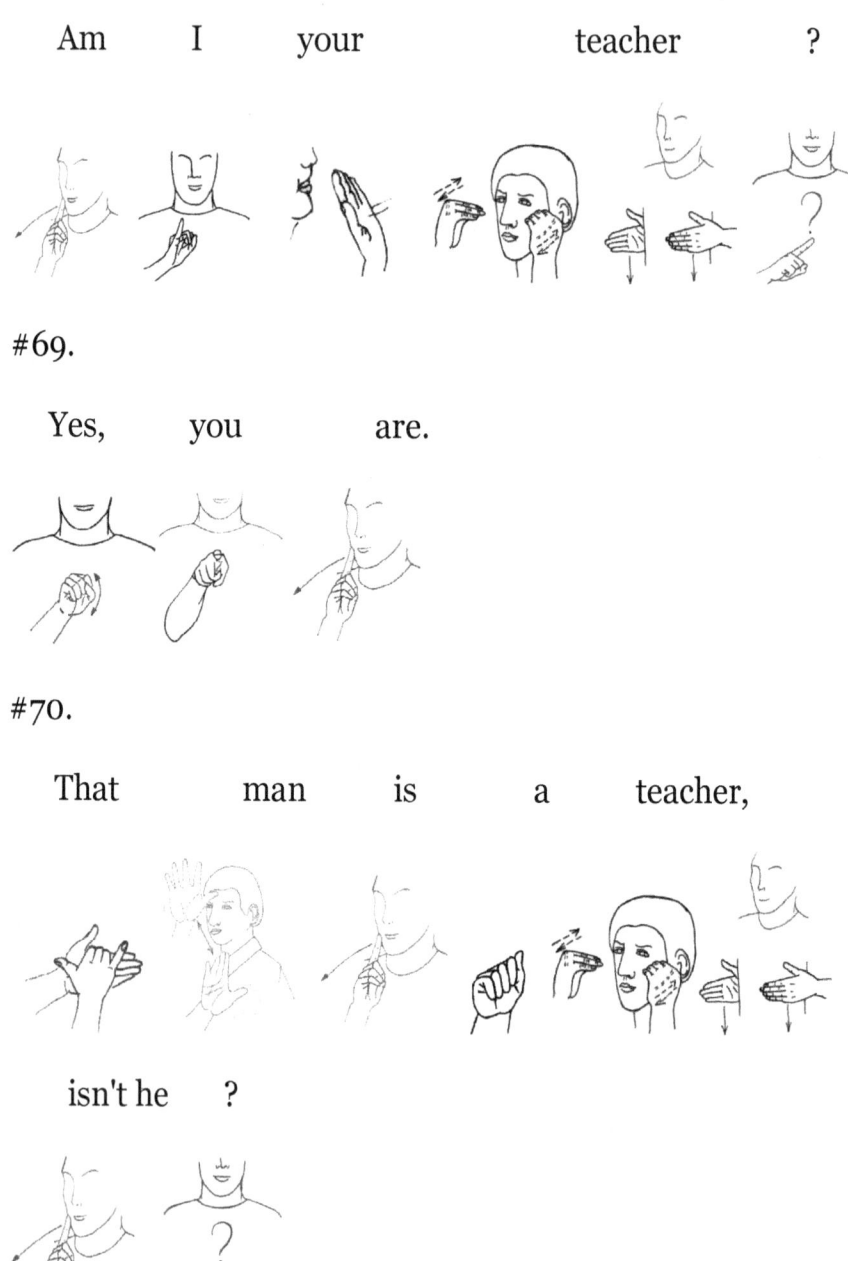

#71.

Yes,        he        is.

#72.

Who        are        those        people.    ?

#73.

Maybe    they        are        farmers.

#74.

Aren't   they        students        ?

29

#75.

I really don't know.

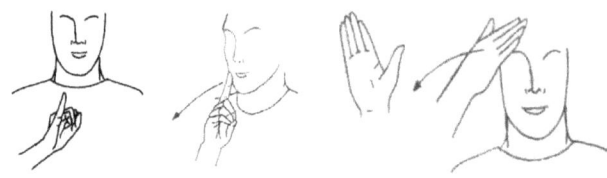

#76.

What is your name ?

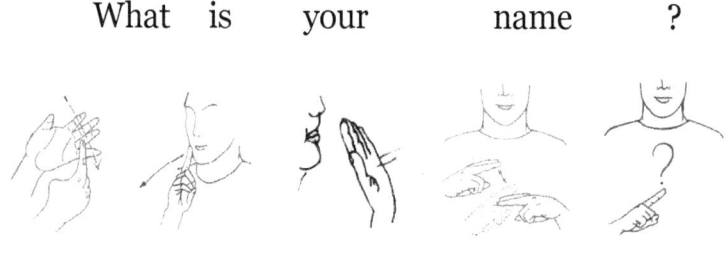

#77.

My name is Jones.

#78.

What is your first name ?

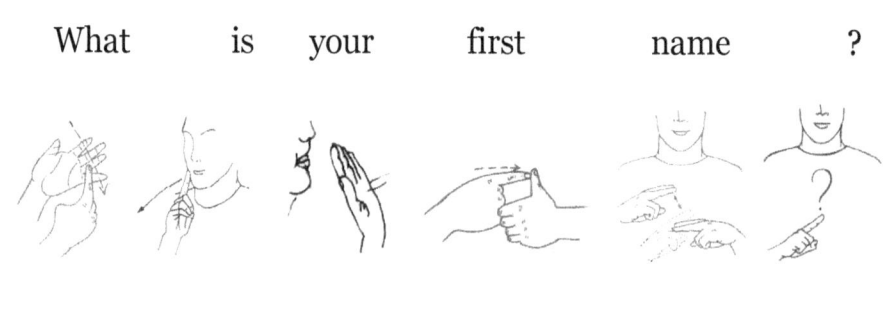

#79.

My          first          name          is          Bill.

#80.

How        do            you          spell    your

last                  name      ?

#81.

J O N E S.

#82.

| What | is | your | friend's | name | ? |

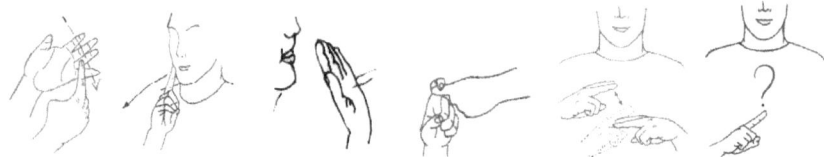

#83.

| His | name | is |

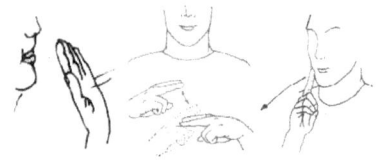

| J o h n | S m i t h. |

#84.

| J o h n | and | I | are | old | friends. |

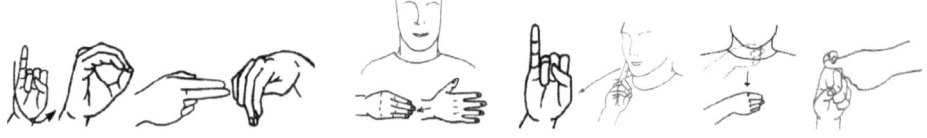

#85.

Are   you   J o h n's   brother ?

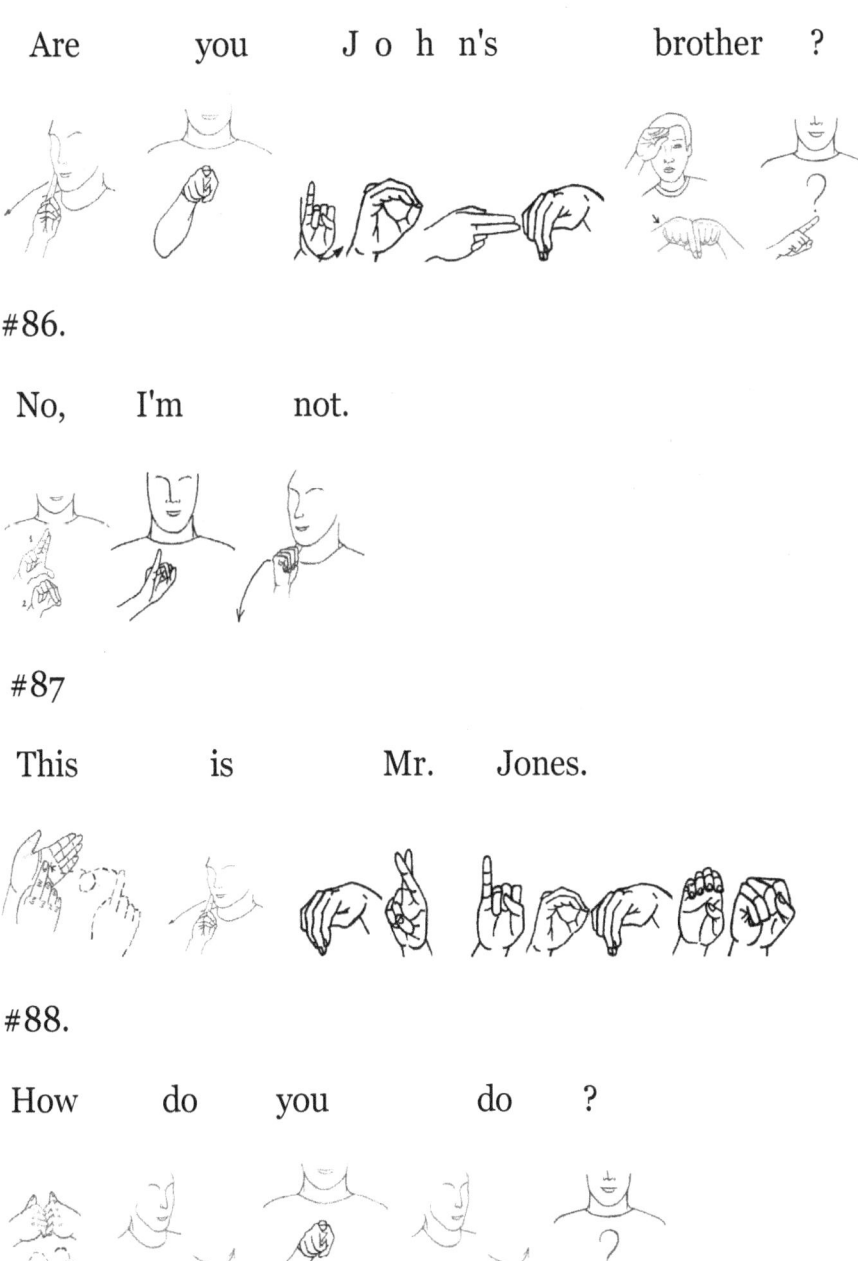

#86.

No,  I'm   not.

#87

This    is    Mr.  Jones.

#88.

How  do  you   do  ?

#89.

Mrs. Jones, this is

Mr. John Smith.

#90.

Very pleased to meet you.

#91.

What day is today ?

#92.

　　　　　Today　　　　　is　　Monday.

#93.

What　　　day　　　was　　　yesterday　　　?

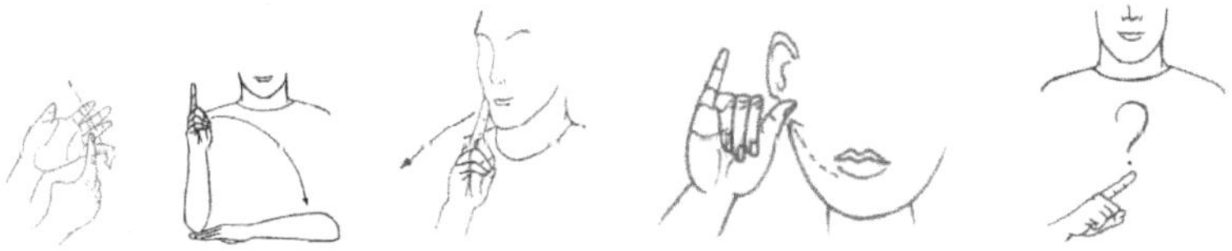

#94.

Yesterday　　　　　was　　Sunday

#95.

What　　day　　　is　　　tomorrow　　?

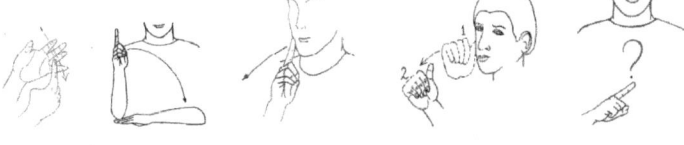

#96.

| What | month | is | this | ? |

#97.

| This | is | January. |

#98.

| Last | month | was | December, | was it | ? |

#99.

| Yes, | it | was. |

#100.

| What | month | is | next | month | ? |
|------|-------|-----|------|-------|---|

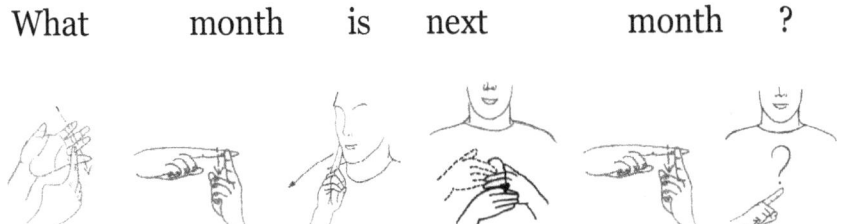

101.

| I | was | in | the | hospital |
|---|-----|-----|-----|----------|

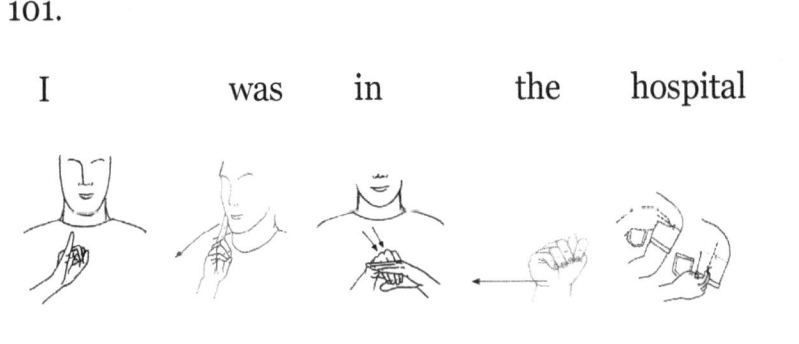

| for | several | weeks. |
|-----|---------|--------|

#102.

| Where | were | you | on | Tuesday | ? |
|-------|------|-----|-----|---------|---|

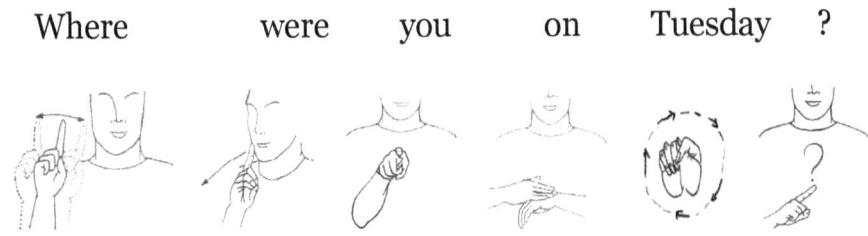

#103.

You were here in February, weren't you ?

#104.

No, I wasn't.

#105.

Your friend was here a week ago,

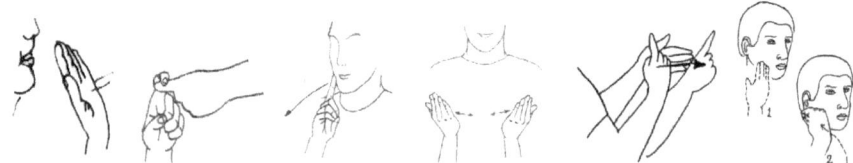

wasn't he ?

#106.

| Do | you | have | a | book | ? |
|---|---|---|---|---|---|

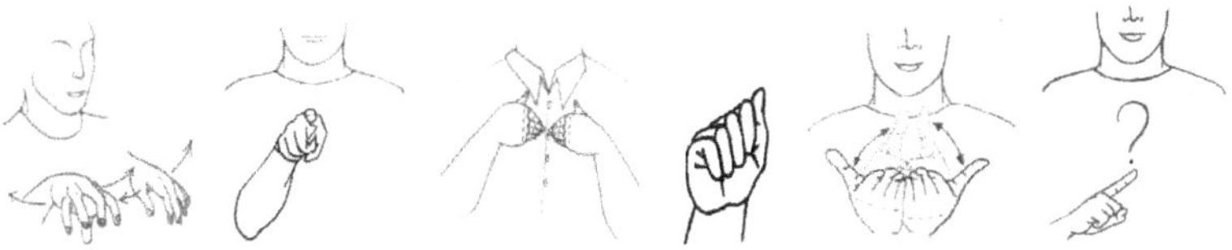

#107.

| Yes, | I | do. |
|---|---|---|

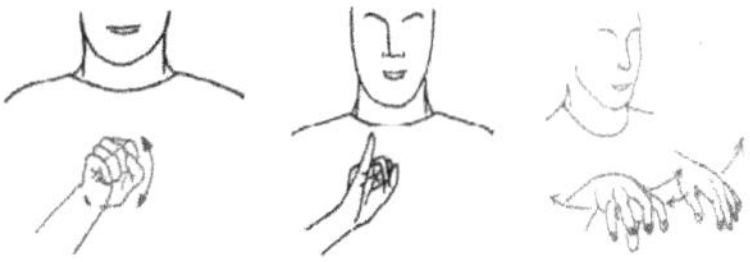

#108.

| You | have | a | radio, | don't | you | ? |
|---|---|---|---|---|---|---|

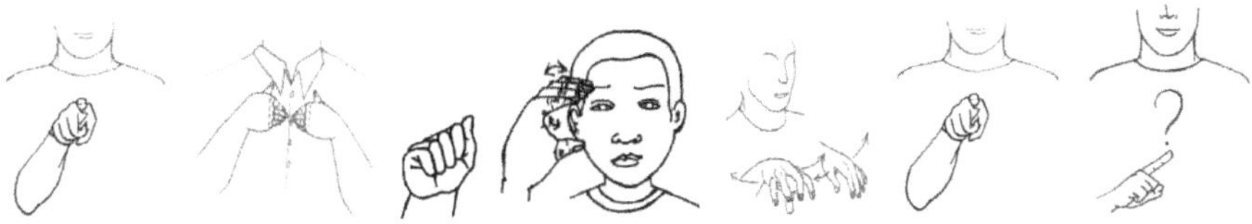

#109.

| No, | I | don't. |
|---|---|---|

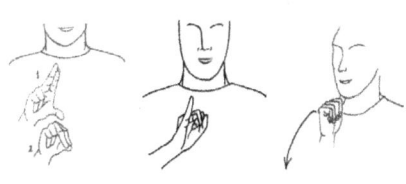

#110.

I      don't     have   a  phonograph,     either.

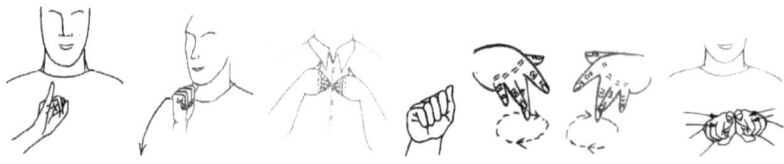

#111.

Does   this     radio    belong      to      you    ?

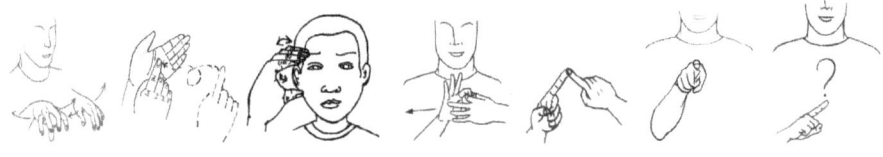

#112.

Yes,      I   think     it   does.

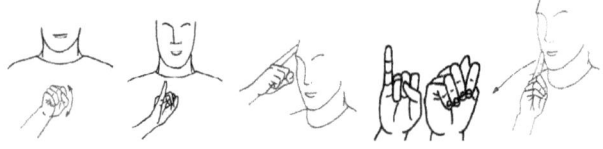

#113.

How many sisters   and   brothers  do  you   have     ?

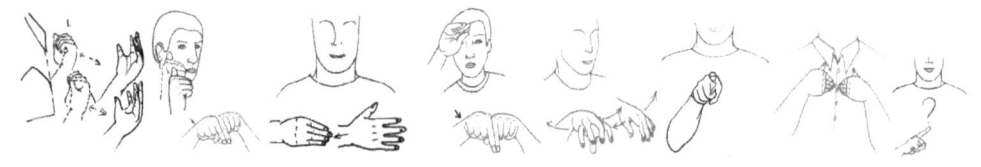

**#114.**

| Don't | you | have | my | hat | ? |
|-------|-----|------|-----|-----|---|

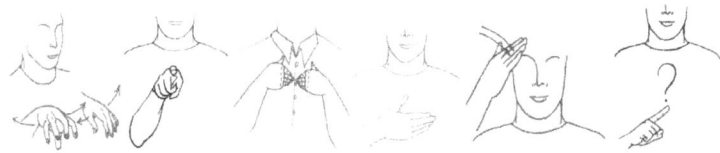

**#115.**

| Yes, | I | have | both | your |
|------|---|------|------|------|

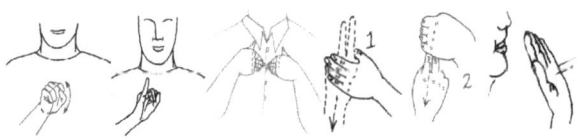

| hat | and | your | coat. |
|-----|-----|------|-------|

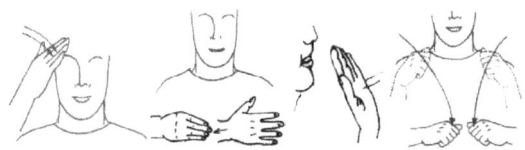

**#116.**

| Does | John | have | a | yellow | pencil | ? |
|------|------|------|---|--------|--------|---|

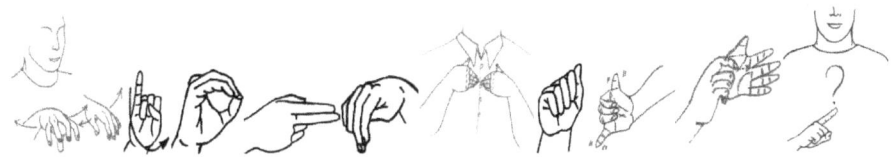

#117.

Yes, he does.

#118.

He has a radio, doesn't he ?

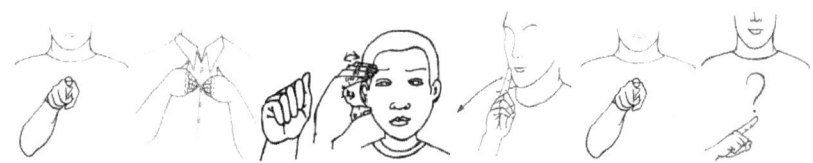

#119.

No, he doesn't have one.

#120.

He    already    has    a phonograph,    but    he

doesn't have.    a    radio    yet.

#121.

What    time    is    it    ?

#122.

It    is    two o'clock.

#123.

It      is      few    minutes after    two.

#124.

My    watch    is    fast    and

your    watch.    is    slow.

#125.

Excuse    me,      can      you      tell    me    the    correct

time    ?

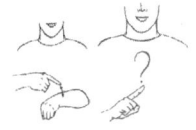

#126.

No,       I      can't.

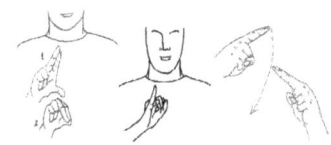

#127.

I    don't know    what    time    it is    now.

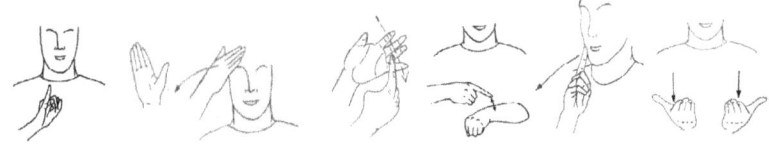

#128.

I don't think it's 4 yet.

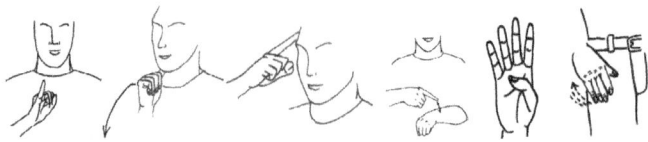

#129.

It must be about three thirty.

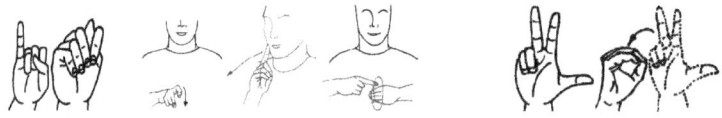

#130.

I get up before time six every day.

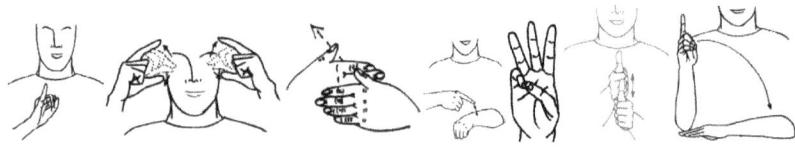

#131.

The restaurant doesn't open until seven forty-five.

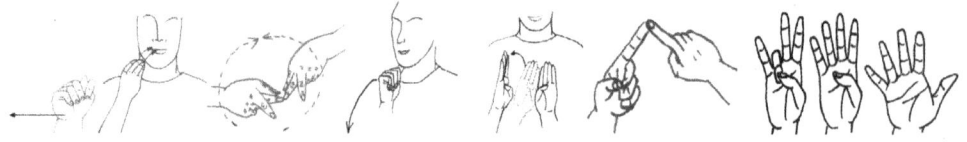

#132.

Will    you    be here    at    ten    tomorrow ?

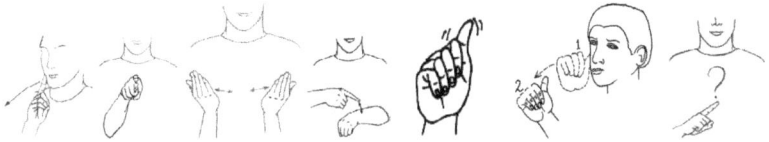

#133.

Yes,    I    will.

#134.

We'll.    be    on    time,    won't we    ?

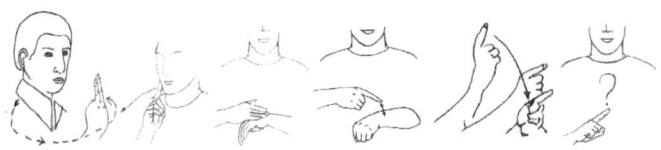

#135.

I    hope    so.

#136.

What's the date today ?

#137.

Today is Nov first, nineteen sixty-three.

#138.

When were you born ?

#139.

I was. born Nov first, nineteen thirty-five.

#140.

Today　　　is　　my　　birthday.

#141.

My　sister　　was　　born　　in.　　nineteen thirty-eight.

#142.

I　　don't know　　the　　exact　　date.

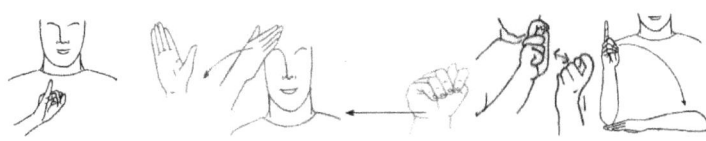

#143.

Where　　were　　you　　born　　?

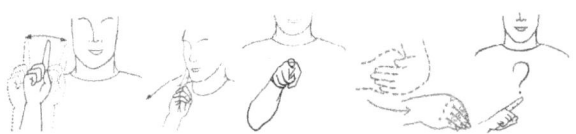

#144.

I          was          born          in          a          little          town

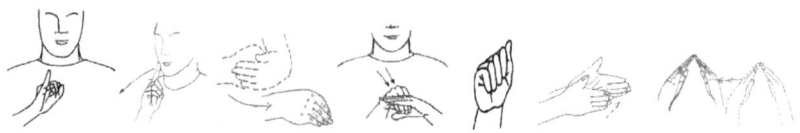

not          far          from    here.

#145.

What    do      you        know.        about.          the

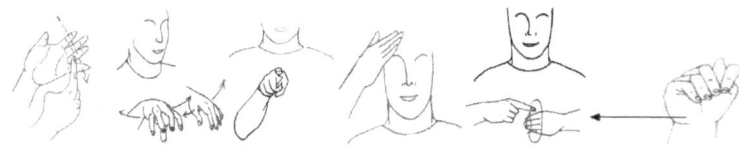

tenth                          century                              ?

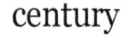

#146.

I          don't know        anything        about        that.

50

#147.

Let's    talk    about   something else.

#148.

Where   were    you  during   the    month    of

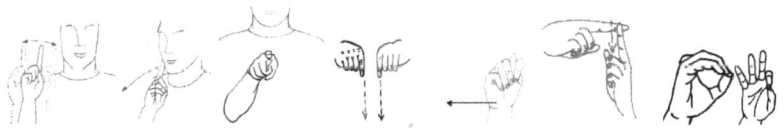

April           last        year      ?

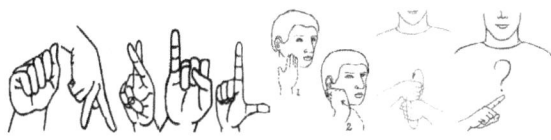

#149.

I     don't  remember   where    I    was then.

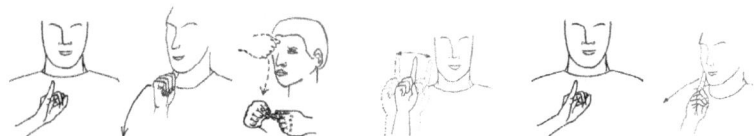

#150.

Where   will   you   be   next   year   at

this   time   ?

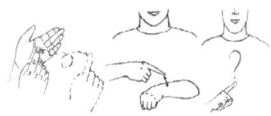

#151.

What   do   you   want   ?

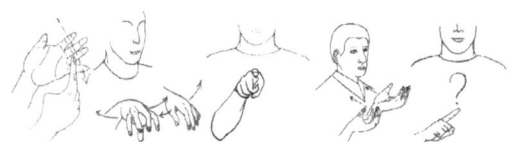

#152.

I   want   a   cup   of   coffee.

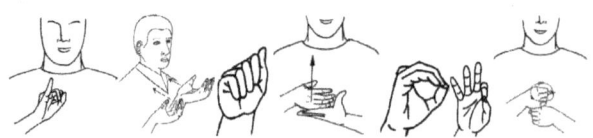

#153.

What would you like to eat ?

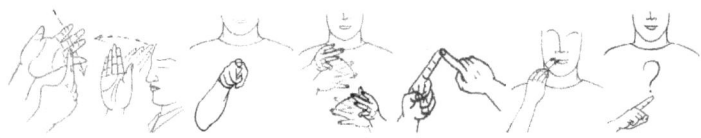

#154.

Please give me a piece of pie.

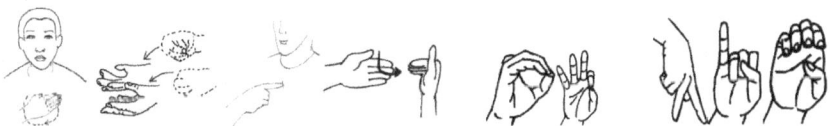

#155.

Which would you like

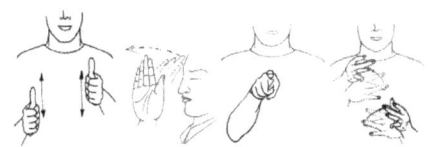

this or that ?

#156.

It   doesn't matter  to     me.

#157.

I  want    to    talk   with    Mr.      Jones

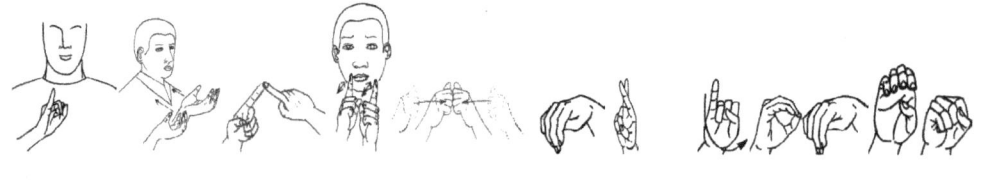

or       Mr.         Smith.

#158.

I   am   sorry, but   both     are  busy right now.

#159.

Would you   like   some   coffee ?

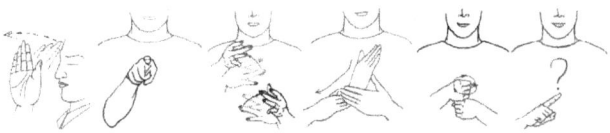

#160.

I  would   rather  have some tea

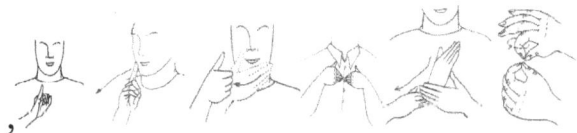

if      you     don't mind.

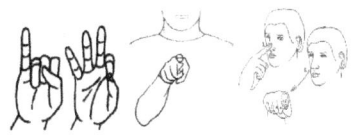

#61.

Do   you    know  any   of    those  people ?

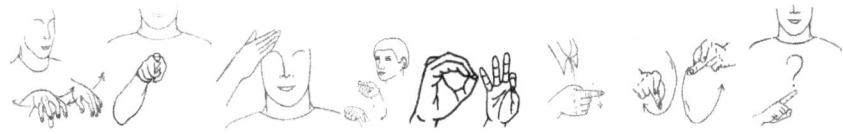

162.

Two or three     of    them look familiar.

#163.

All     of    those. people are   friends of.    mine.

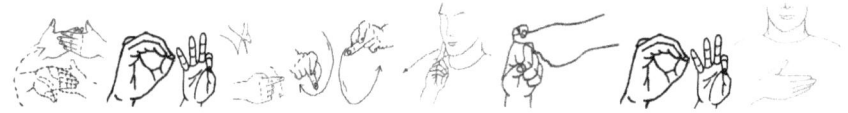

#164.

Which    one   of     those    men     is

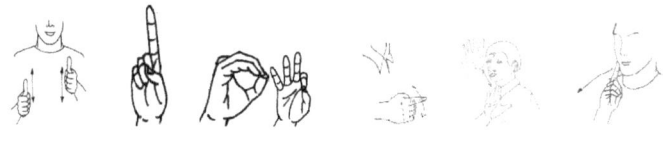

    Mr.        Taylor           ?

#165.

   Is    he    the   tall man   on    the      left     ?

#166.

Do   you      speak   English ?

#167.

Yes,      a little.

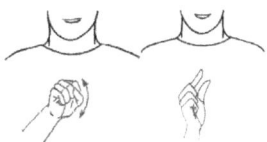

#168.

Does   your   friend   speak   English. ?

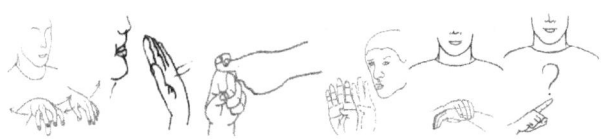

#169.

Yes,   he   speaks English perfectly.

#170.

What    is    his  native  language ?

#171.

I  don't know  what  his    native language is.

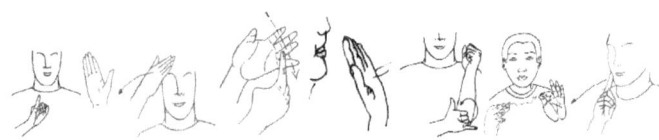

#172.

How  many  languages do you speak    ?

#173.

My    friend    reads    and    writes  several languages.

#174.

How  well  do  you  know  French  ?

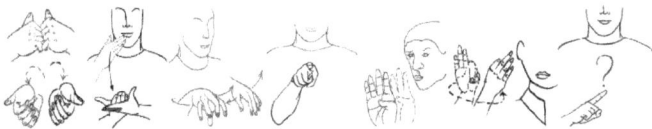

#175.

He speaks French  with  American  accent.

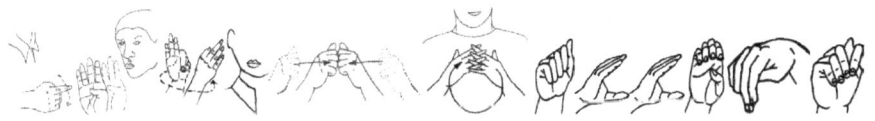

#176.

My.  parents  speak  English fluently.

#177.

Mr.  Jones  can  read

French  pretty well.

#178.

Sometimes   I    make    mistakes   when   I

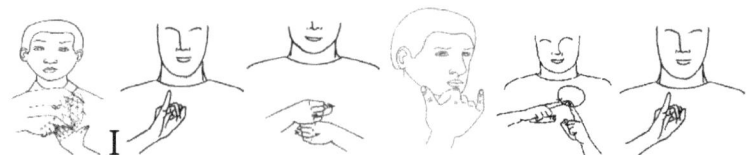

speak English.

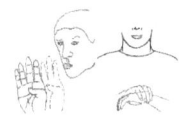

#179.

I       have    a lot   of trouble  with  pronunciation.

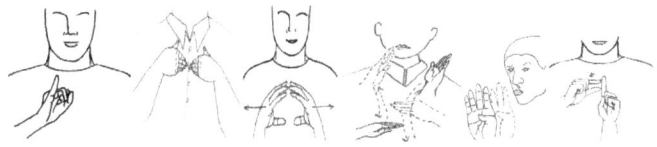

#180.

How      is   her    accent    in    French   ?

#181.

What   are   you   doing   ?

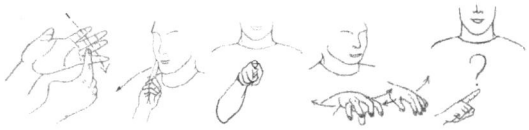

#182.

I    am    reading   a book.

#183.

What   is your   friend   doing.   ?

#184.

He   is studying his lesson.

#185.

I am not doing anything right now.

#186.

Where are you going ?

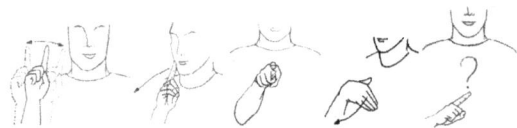

#187.

I am going home.

#188.

What time are you coming back ?

#189.

I    am not sure  what time I     am   coming back.

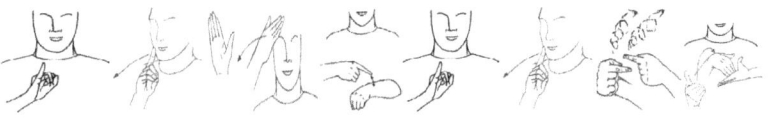

#190.

What    are    you    thinking about    ?

#191.

I     am     thinking about my lesson.

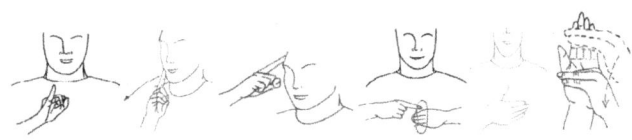

#192.

Who    are  you    writing    to ?

#193.

I    am    writing to  to  a friend   of    mine

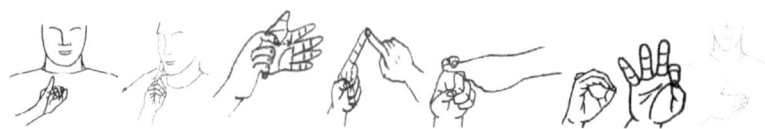

in    South    America.

#194.

Who    are    you    waiting  for    ?

#195.

I 'm    not    waiting for    any  body.

#196.

How    old    are  you  ?

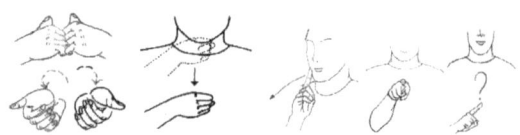

#197.

I        am twenty-one years old.

#198.

My  brother  is    not quite  twenty-five.

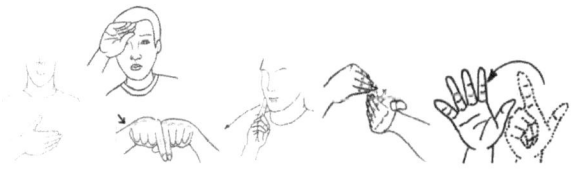

#199.

                John                is      not   forty-five        yet,

        is      he            ?

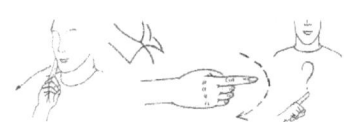

#200.

Mr.       Smith           is  still in his      fifties.

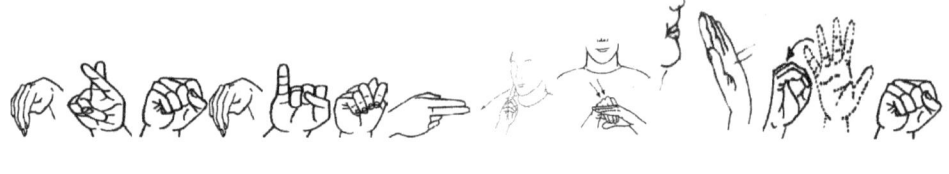

#201.

I   am  two  years  older  than   you are.

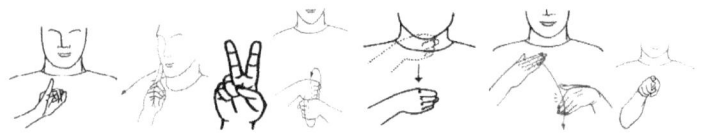

#202.

My   brother  is  two  years younger than  I   am .

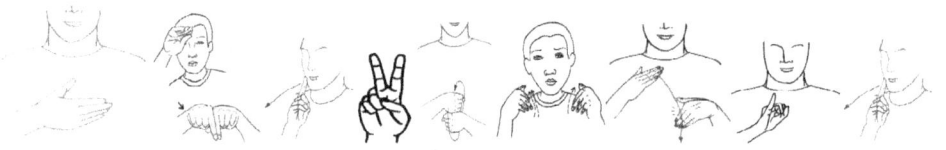

#203.

How   many   are   in   your  family  ?

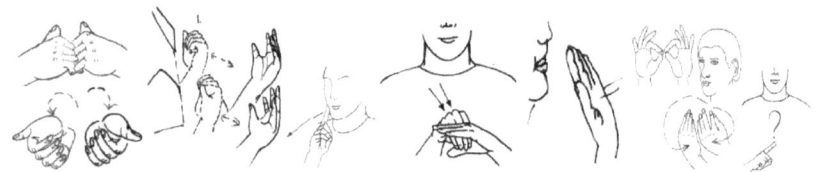

#204.

There    are  seven of   us   altogether.

#205.

My   sister      is     oldest.

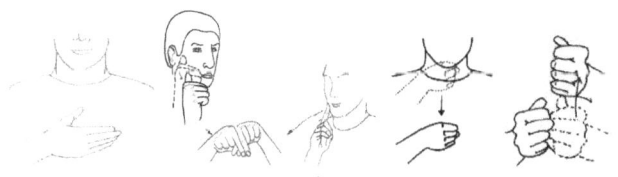

#206.

I   am   the   youngest.

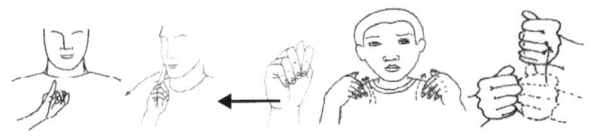

#207.

Guess how  old   I   am.

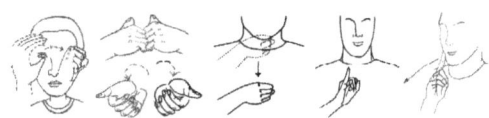

#208.

I say you are about twenty-three.

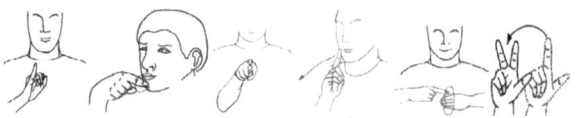

#209.

I was thirty on my last birthday.

#210.

I will be sixty-one next Tuesday

#211.

What time do you get up everyday ?

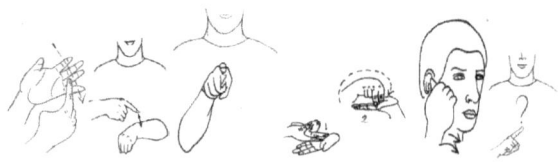

#212.

I   usually   wake   up early.

#213.

I  get up  at 6 o'clock everyday.

#214.

My. brother  gets up  later  than  I do.

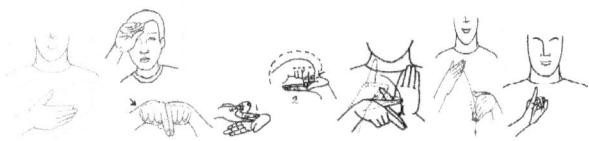

#215.

After I   get dressed, I   have   breakfast

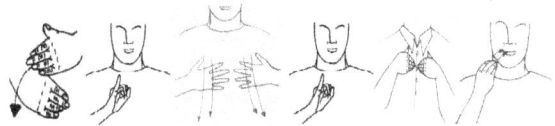

#216.

Usually, I have big breakfast.

#217.

I have juice, cereal, toast,

and coffee for breakfast.

#218.

I leave the house eight a.m. each day.

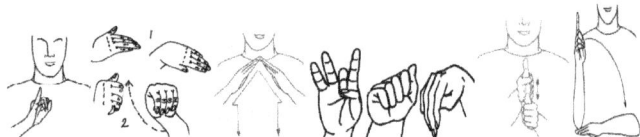

#219.

I   get      to   work   at   nine    every    morning.

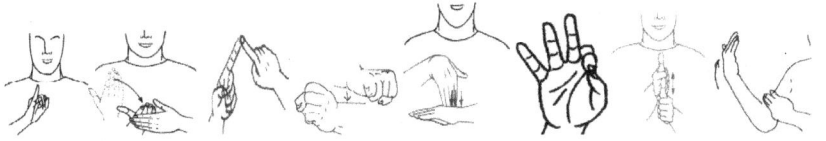

#220.

I    work    hard    all    morning.

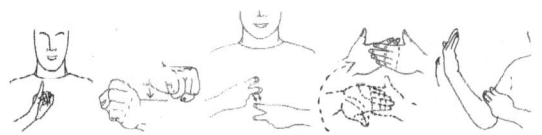

#221.

I    go   out   for    lunch   about 12:30.

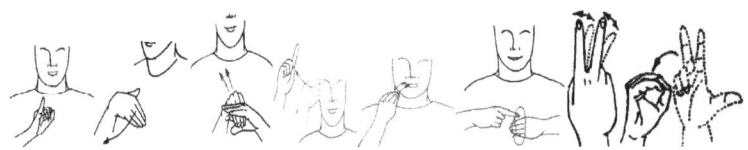

#222.

I    finish    working at        5:45

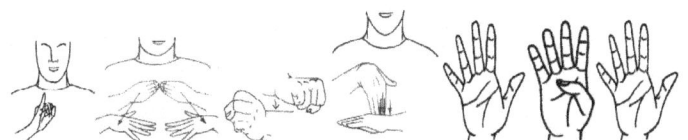

#223.

I　　eat　dinner　about　7

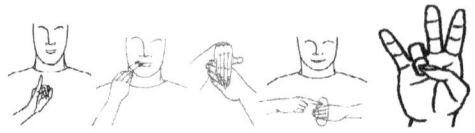

#224.

Before　I　　eat　　　dinner, I　　read　the newspaper for awhile.

#225.

I　　usually　go　　to　bed　　about　midnight.

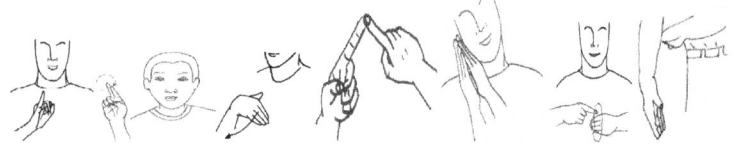

#226.

What　time　did　you　　get up　yesterday　morning?

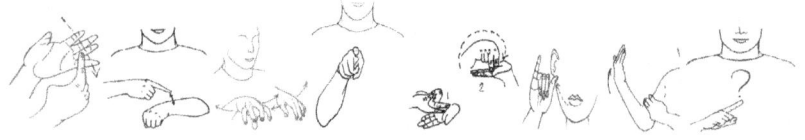

#227.

I   woke  up early  and  got up  6 o'clock.

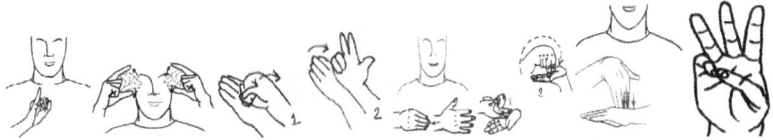

#228.

My brother got up  earlier     than  I  did.

#229.

Did   you  get  dressed right away ?

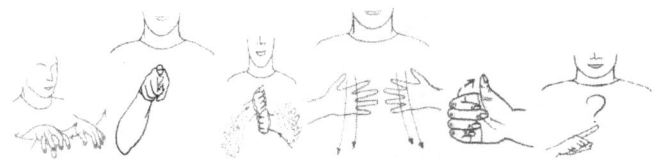

#230.

Yes,   I   got dressed  and   had   breakfast.

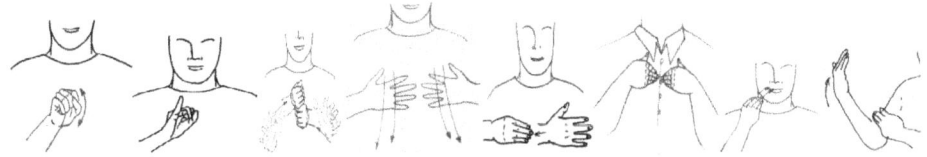

#231.

What    kind    breakfast    did    you    have    ?

#232.

What    time    did    you    get to work yesterday morning ?

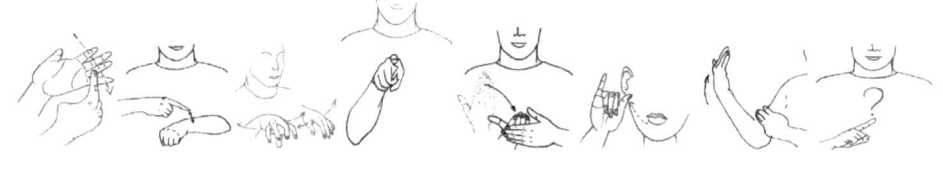

#233.

I        left        the    house    at    8 o'clock and    got

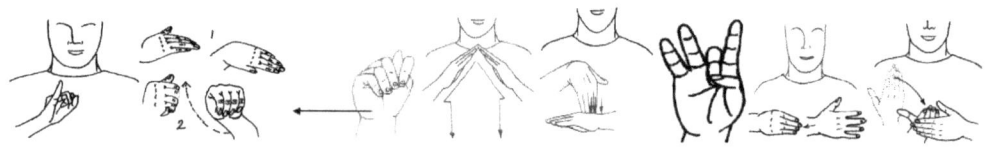

to    work    at        8:30.

#234.

Did    you.   work   all        day      ?

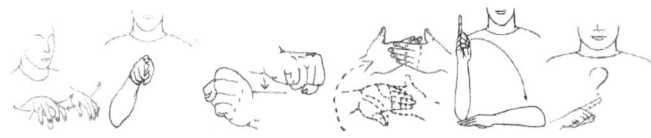

#235.

Yes,        I      worked  from  early    morning until

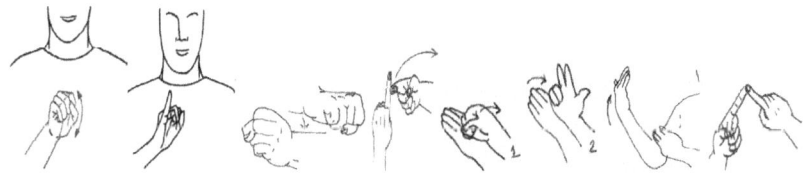

late         at         night.

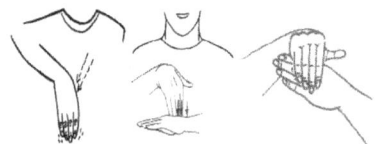

#236.

At        noon      I     had   lunch      with

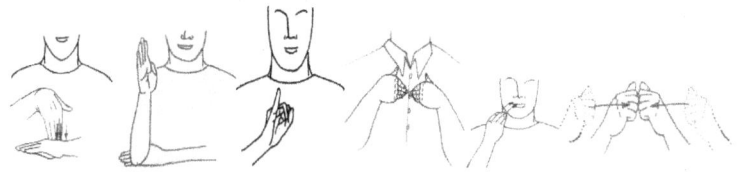

a   friend.  of    mine.

#237.

I    finished    working    at    5:30    and

went    home.

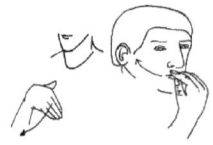

#238.

After    dinner    I    read    a magazine   and

made    some    telephone calls.

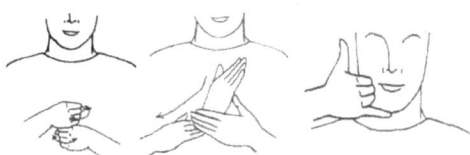

#239.

I    went   to     bed      at      11:30    p.m.

#240.

I   went   to    sleep immediately and   slept

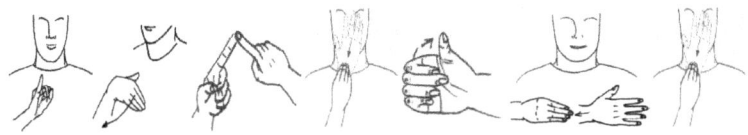

soundly   all    night.

#241.

Where    did    you     go    yesterday ?

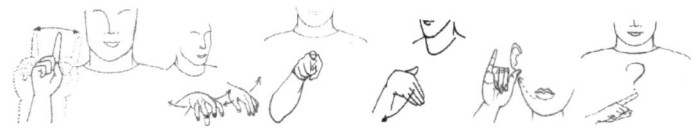

#242.

I   went   to    see   a friend   of    mine.

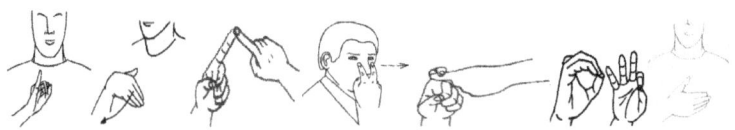

#243.

Did    you    see    Mr.       Jones           ?

#244.

   I   didn't   see   Mr.      Jones,

but    I    saw      John        Smith.

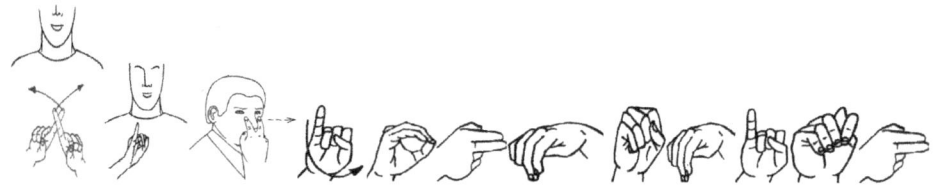

#245.

What   did   you   talk   about   ?

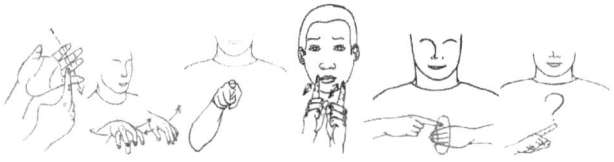

#246.

We     talked     about     a lot     of things.

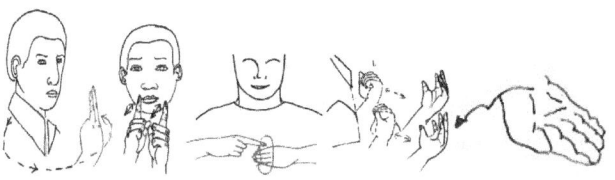

#247.

I     asked     him     lot of     questions.

#248.

What     did     you     ask     him     ?

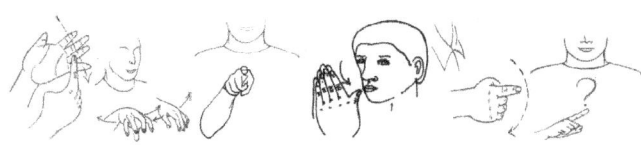

#249.

I     asked     him     if     he     spoke.     English.

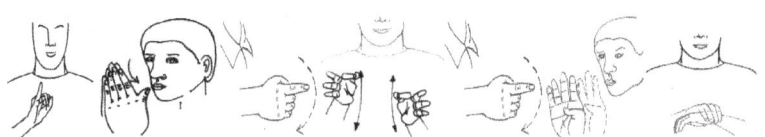

#250.

He    said   he     spoke  a little  English.

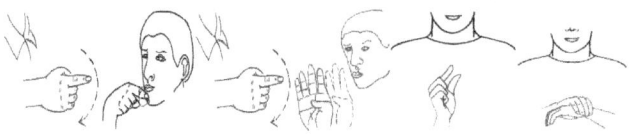

#251.

Then   I   asked   him   if    he   knew   anybody

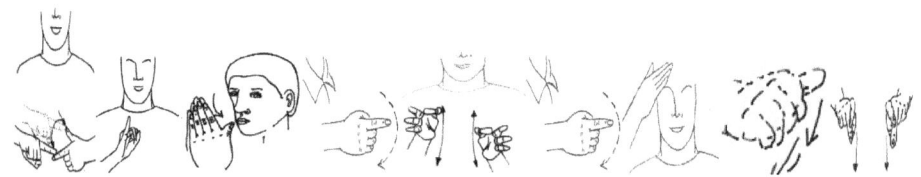

in    New York.

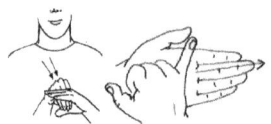

#252.

He    said   he   knew  a lot   people  there.

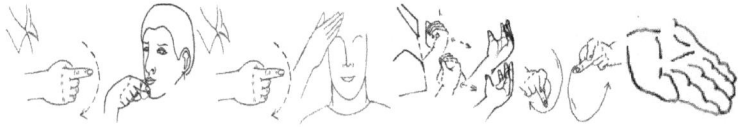

#253.

Finally, I asked him how old he was.

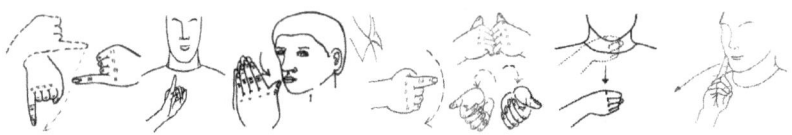

#254.

He said he rather not tell his age.

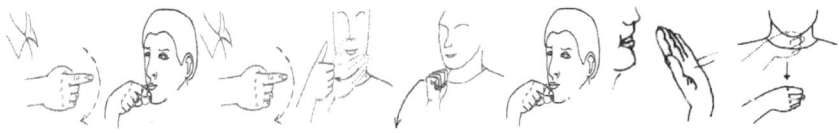

#255.

He answered almost all my questions.

#256.

What time   did   you        use        get up

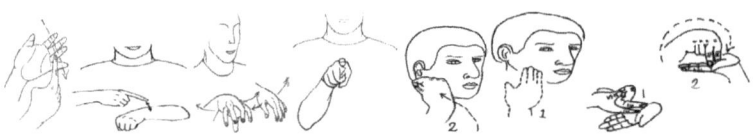

last       year   ?

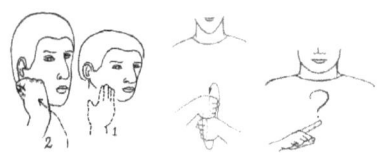

#257.

I    used to    wake up         early         and

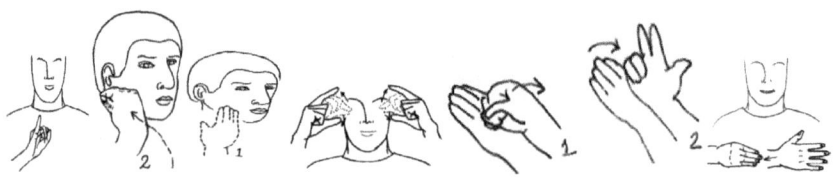

get up      at        7 o'clock

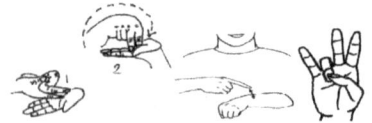

#258.

I   used      to   set   my   alarm   for exactly

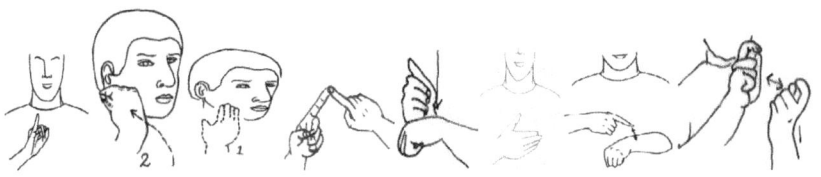

7    a.m.

#259.

I   never   used      to      oversleep.

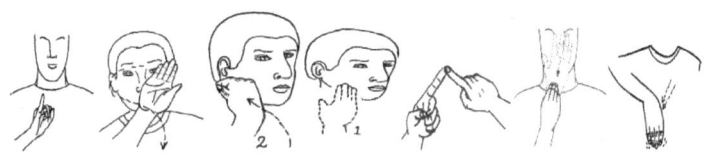

#260.

I   used to    get dressed   quickly   every   morning.

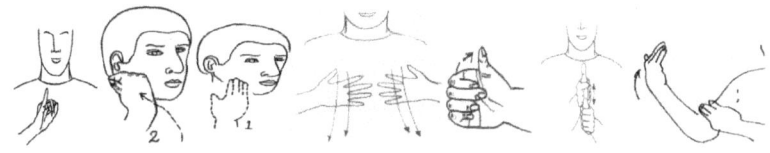

#261.

I  always  used to  leave  for

work  at  8:30.

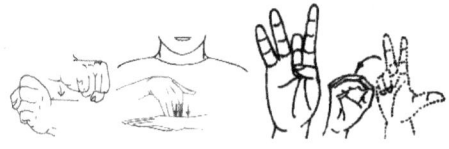

#262.

I  used  to  start  working  at

9:00  everyday.

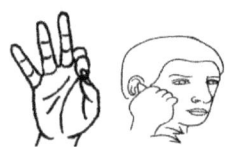

#263.

I  used  to    lunch  at the same time.

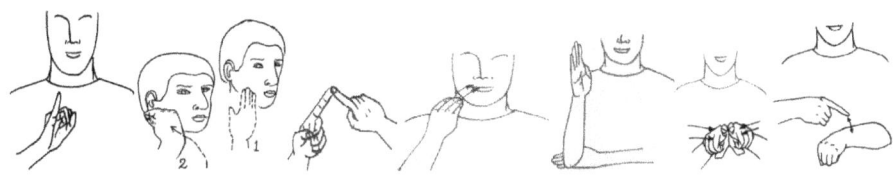

#264.

I  used  to  work  until  nearly

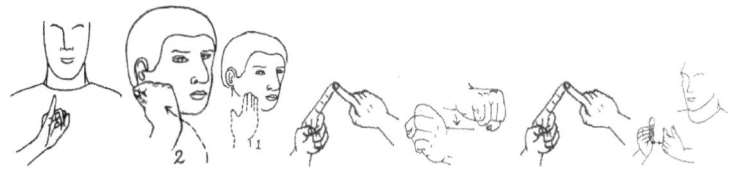

6:00 o'clock each day.

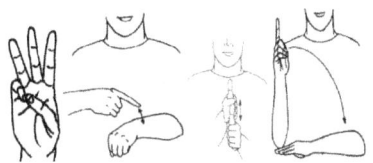

#265.

I  used  to  have dinner at  7:30

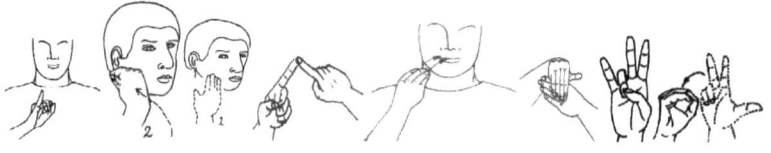

and  go  to  bed  early.

#266.

Brother  and  I  used  to  go to

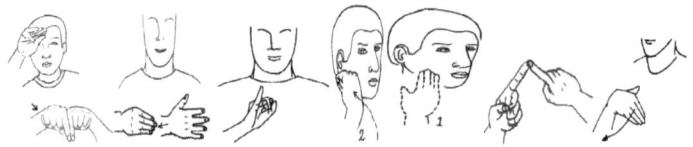

many  places  together.

#267.

We   used to   go   to   movies   once   a week.

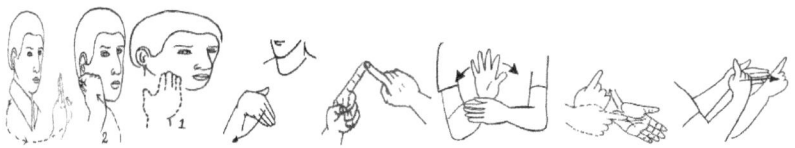

#268.

We   used   to   have many   interesting   friends.

#269.

My   brother   used   to.   speak French   to   me.

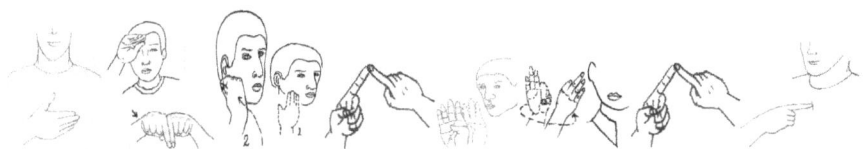

#270.

I   always   used to   ask   him   lot   of questions.

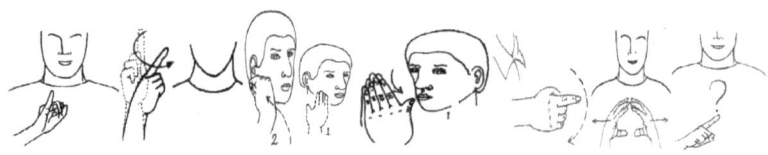

#271.

Where   do   you   live   ?

#272.

I   live   on   Washington   Street.

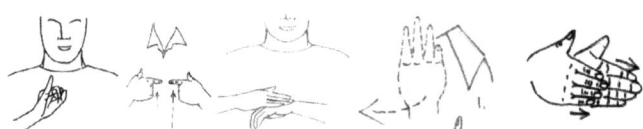

#273.

What's   your   address ?

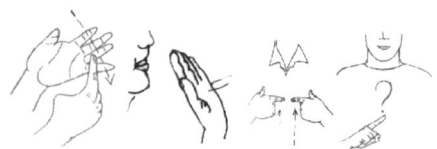

#274.

I    live.    at        203        Washington  Street.

#275.

I    am        Mr.        Smith's                next    door neighbor.

#276.

You  live  here    in        the    city,  don't you  ?

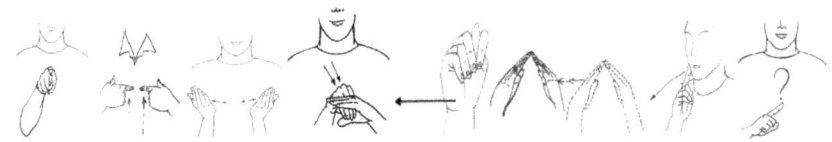

#277.

I    am    from    out    of        town.

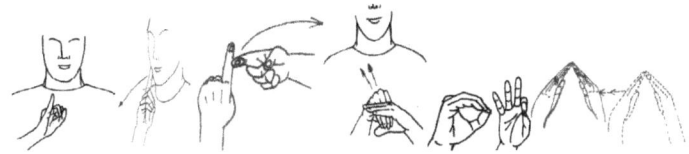

#278.

How    long    have    you   lived    here   ?

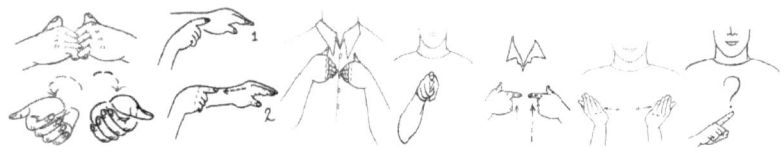

#279.

I    have    lived    here    for    five    years.

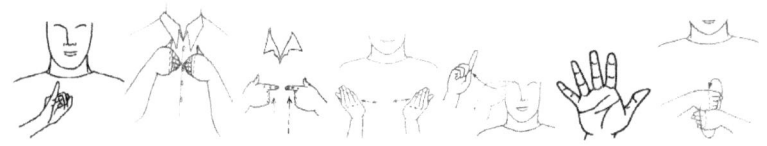

#280.

He's   known    me    for    over    ten   years.

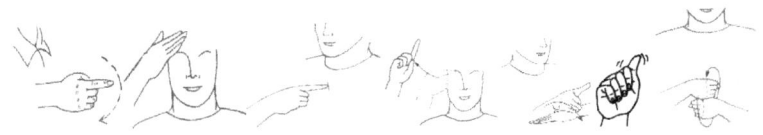

#281.

I    have    spoken English   all   my    life.

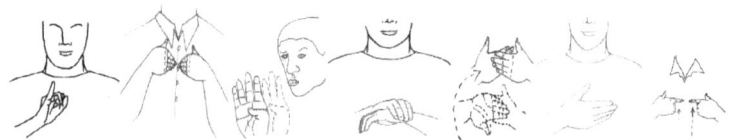

#282.

I    already   read   that   book.

#283.

Has    he    studied French   very    long        ?

#284.

Have   you    had    breakfast        ?

#285.

Yes,    I    had   breakfast    two   hours   ago.

#286.

Where    were   you yesterday afternoon ?

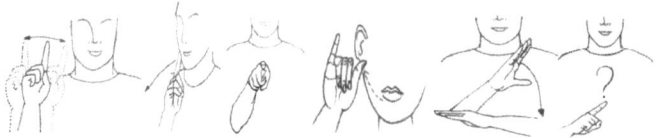

#287.

   I    was    at    home    all    afternoon.

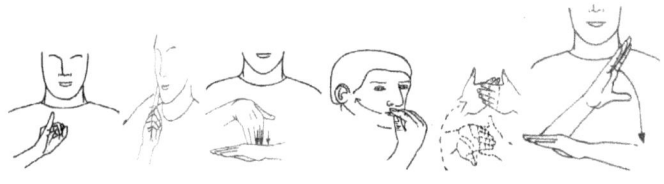

#288.

   I    was    writing some letters    to    friends of    mine.

#289.

What were you doing at about 4 o'clock yesterday

afternoon ?

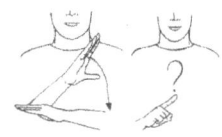

#290.

I was listening to the radio.

#291.

What were you doing when I telephoned you ?

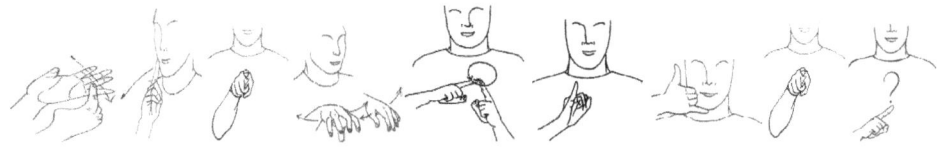

#292.

When    you    called    me,    I    was    eating dinner.

#293.

When    I    saw    Mr.    Jones,

he    was    talking with    John.

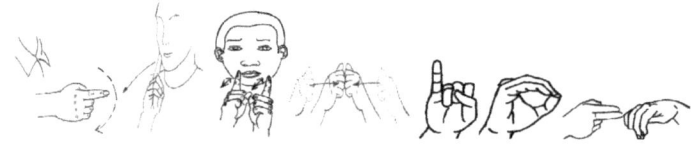

Smith.

#294.

While    you  were writing letters,     I    was

reading    a book.

#295.

While   you  having breakfast, John

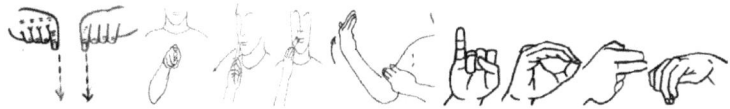

was talking on   the telephone.

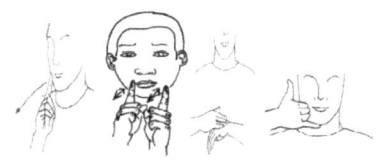

#296.

Can  you  guess    what    I  was  doing this  morning  ?

#297.

I    can't    remember  what      John          was

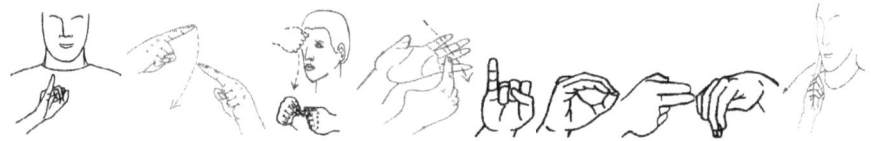

doing   yesterday  afternoon.

#298.

I've    forgotten   what   he      said   his    address   was.

#299.

I've   forgotten    what  time  he     said    he    had  dinner

last        night.

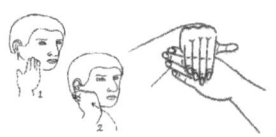

#300.

They  called    just as   we    were     having   dinner.

#301.

What  color   is   your       book      ?

#302.

My.    book.    has    a dark    blue.        cover.

#303.

How  much does  that          typewriter            weigh

?

#304.

It       is      not    too heavy, but

I      don't   know the exact  weight.

#305.

This      round            table   weighs  about forty-five

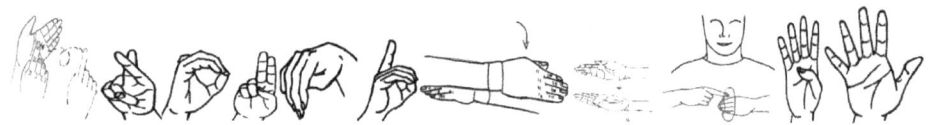

pounds.

#306.

What  size  suitcase  do    you    own   ?

#307.

One    of   my   suitcases is   small, and    the   other

one   is   medium size.

#308.

I    like   the     shape      of

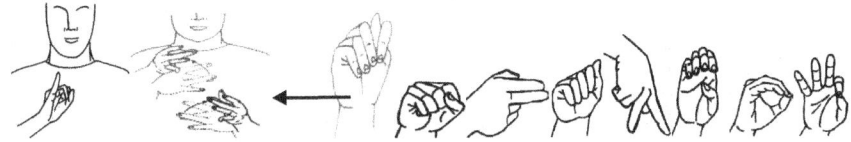

that   table.

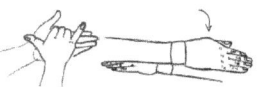

#309.

How   long    is    Jones    Boulevard.  ?

#310.

That   street   is   only   two            miles .

#311.

Will    you   please   measure this   window  to

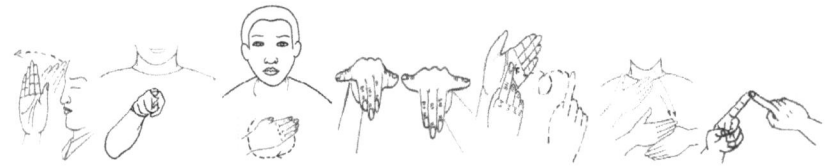

see.   how    wide.    it     is   ?

#312.

This   window is   as    wide  as that   one.

#313.

The    walls    are three  inches   thick.

#314.

This   material   feels    soft.

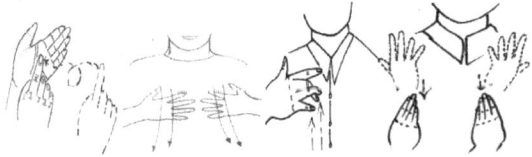

315.

This    pencil  is   longer    than   that one.

#316.

Would you please     tell  Mr.     Cooper

I'm  here  ?

#317.

Take these  books home with  you   tonight.

#318.

Please  bring   me those  magazines.

#319.

Would you help. me lift this heavy box

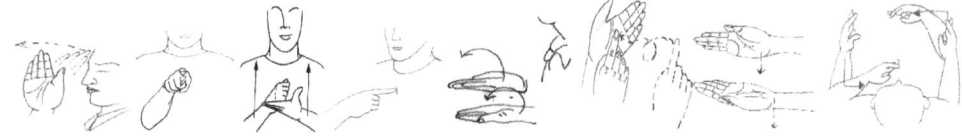

?

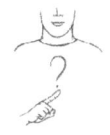

#320.

Please ask John to. turn off the lights.

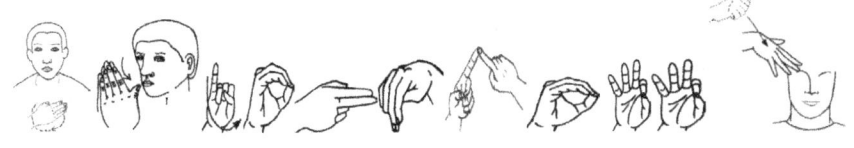

#321.

Put your books down on the table.

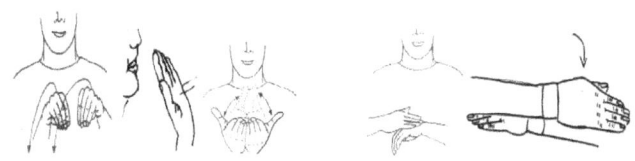

#322.

Get   me   hammer  from  kitchen, will   you    ?

#323.

Hang  my  coat   in    closet, will      you please  ?

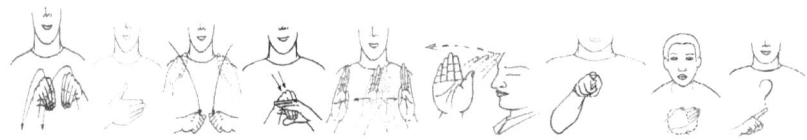

#324.

Please. don't  bother    me   now  I'm    very    busy.

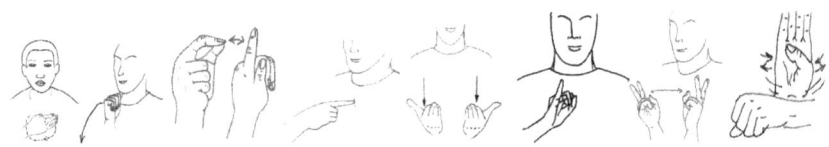

#325.

Would you    mind  mailing  this   letter  for     me   ?

#326.

If    you   have   time,  will   you    call    me   tomorrow

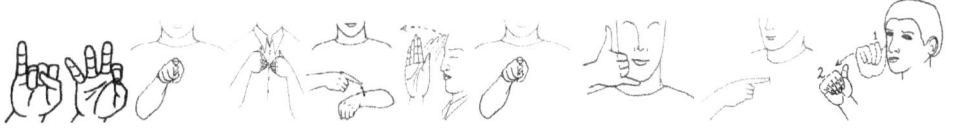

?

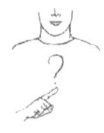

#327.

Please, pick up those   cups   and   saucers.

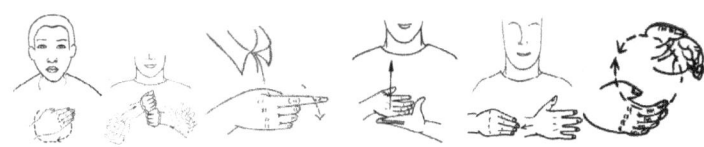

#328.

Will   you  do   me  a favor ?

#329.

Please count the chairs in that room.

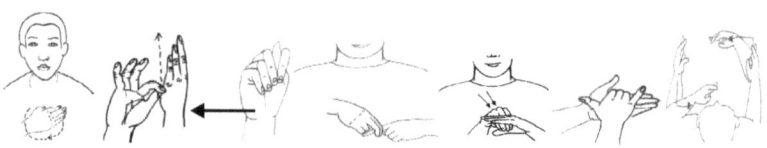

# 330.

Please pour this milk into that glass.

#331.

Excuse me, sir Can you give me some

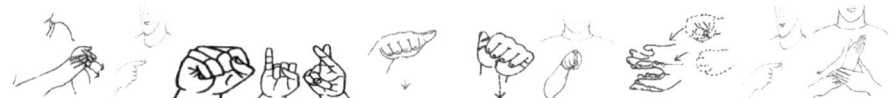

information ?

#332.

Can you tell where is Peach Street ?

#333.

It     is two  blocks  straight ahead.

#334.

Which  direction is   to      movie     theater  ?

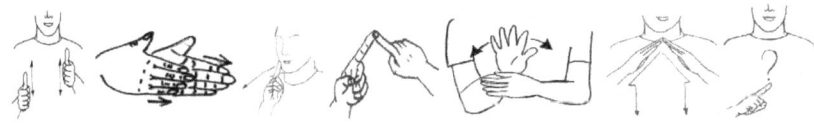

#335.

Turn  right  at     next        corner.

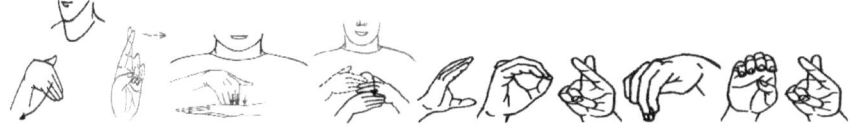

#336.

How     far is it  to    the.   university  ?

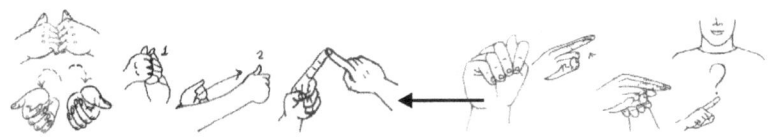

#337.

It.     is a  long     way     from     here.

#338.

The     school is     around     the          corner.

#339.

The. restaurant     is     across  the street  from  the hotel.

#340.

You   can't     miss     it.

**#341.**

Do    you    happen    to    know

Mr.                Cooper's                    telephone ?

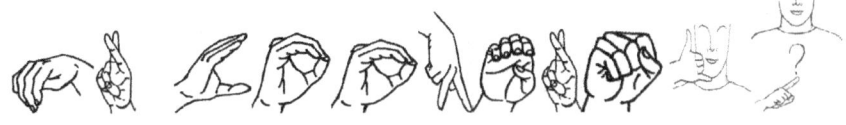

**#342.**

Could  you tell  me   where   is    nearest telephone ?

**#343.**

Should      I        go    this      way,        or

that      way        ?

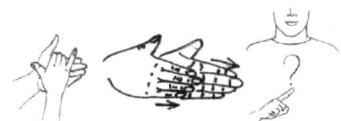

#344.

Go    that    way    for    two    blocks,

then    turn left.

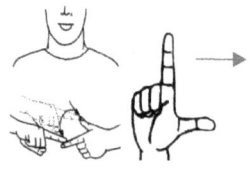

#345.

Excuse.    me;    is    this    seat    taken    ?

#346.

Are    you    married    ?

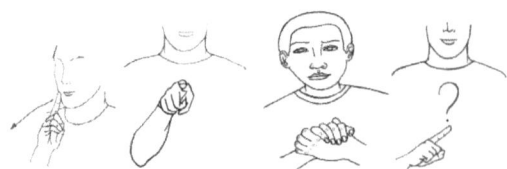

110

#347.

No, I'm not married I am single.

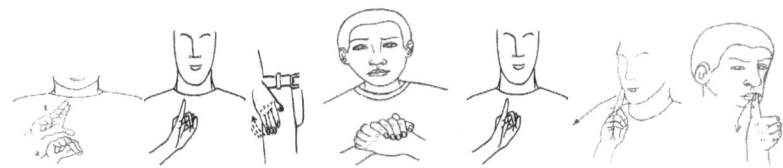

#348.

Your niece is engaged, true ?

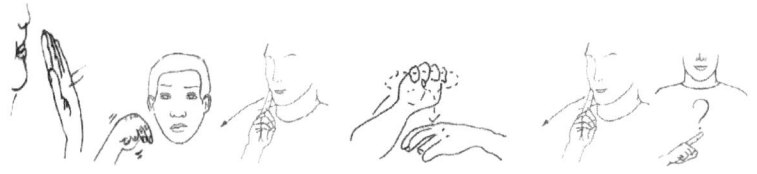

#349.

My sister has been engaged for two months.

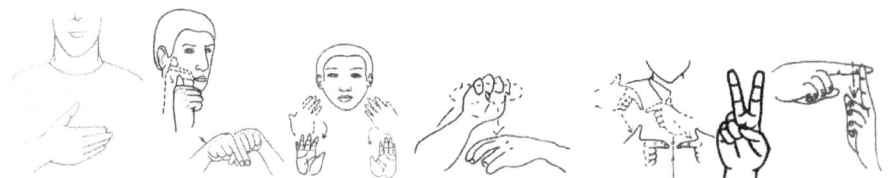

#350.

My. grandfather married in 1921.

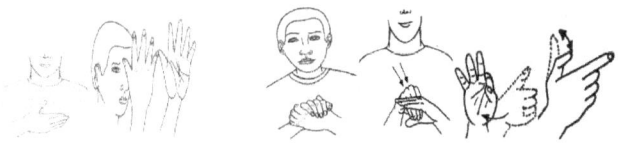

#351.

When   is   your grandparents' wedding   anniversary ?

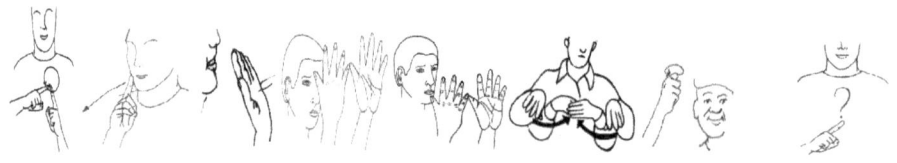

#352.

How   long they      been   married   ?

#353.

They've   been   married   for   quite a few years.

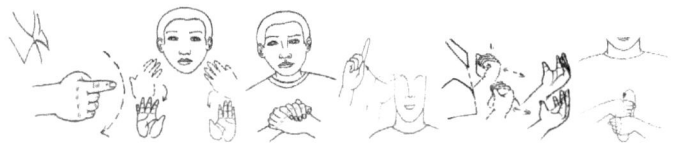

#354.

Who   did         George              marry   ?

#355.

Do they      have children ?

#356.

They      had      a baby last     month.

#357.

My   son   to   get   married   in     June.

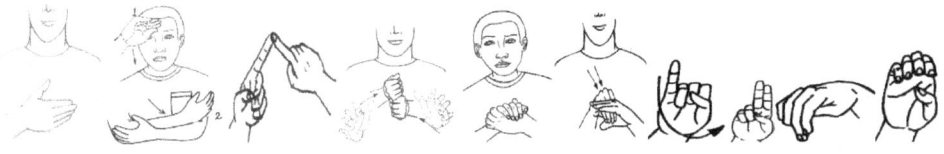

#358.

They.   don't know   when   the   wedding will   be.

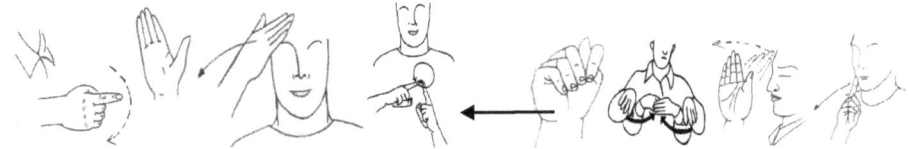

#359.

Their grand children    grown now.

#360.

She's    widow.                Her husband died last    year.

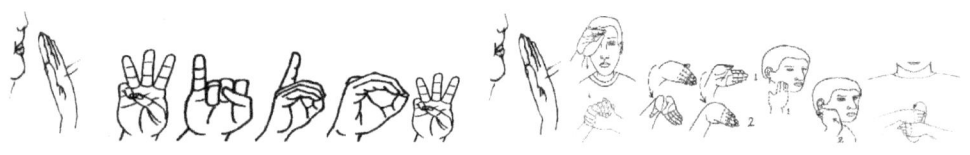

#361.

Where    did    you.    grow up ?

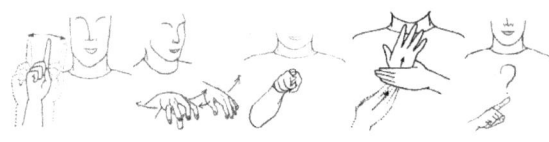

#362.

I    grew up    here    in    this    neighborhood.

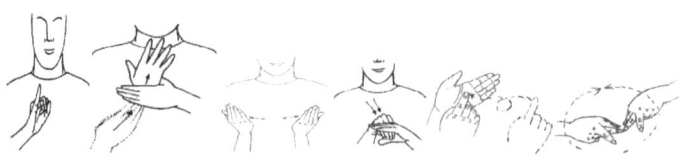

#363.

My  friend  spent.  his  childhood  in  California.

#364

He  lived  in  California until  he  was seventeen.

#365.

There have been  a lot of changes here  in  the last  20  years.

#366.

There  was a grocery store  on the  corner.

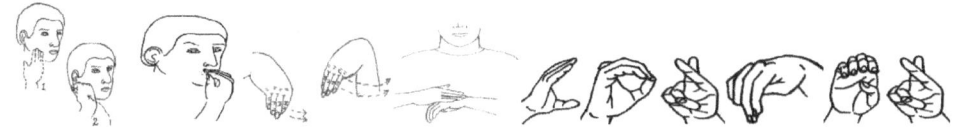

#367.

All of those houses were built.   in the last ten   years.

#368.

They   are   building a new   house up the street   from me.

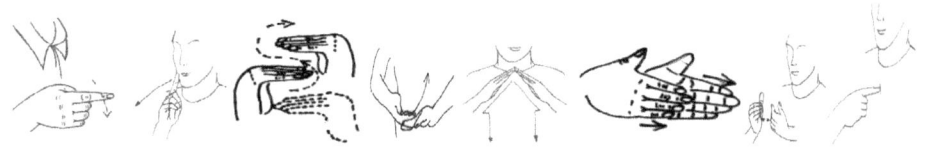

#369.

If   you   build   that   home,   will   you

spend   forever your life   there   ?

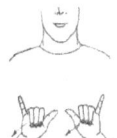  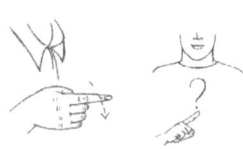

#370.

Are   your   neighbors   very   friendly     ?

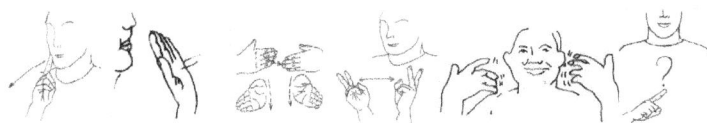

#371.

We      know      all         very      good.

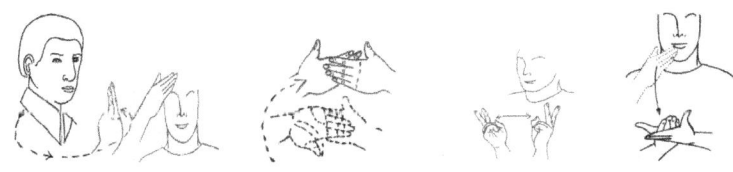

#372.

A young married couple   moved    in    next door  to us.

#373.

Who  bought   that   new   house on the street   near   you   ?

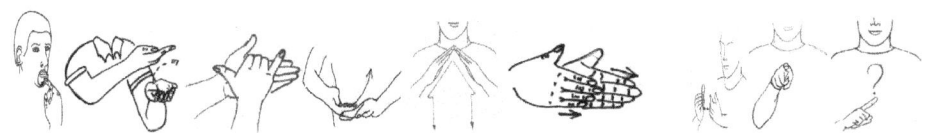

#374.

An elderly man    rented    the    big   white   house.

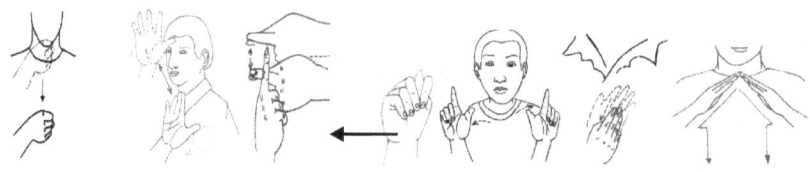

#375.

     Beautiful trees those are!

#376.

What  time    are   you                    wake up tomorrow morning  ?

#377.

  I    will   wake up   early    and    get up at 6:30.

#378.

What will you do then ?

#379.

After I get dressed, I will have breakfast.

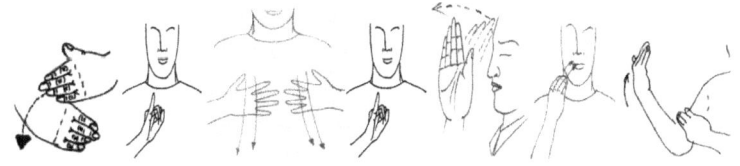

#380.

What will you have f or breakfast tomorrow ?

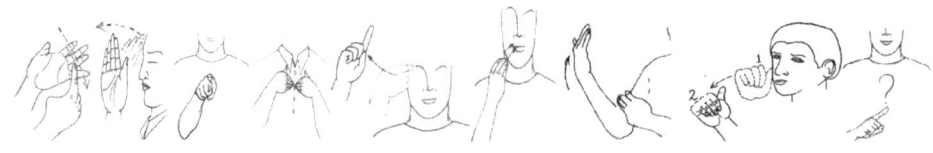

#381.

I will probably have eggs and toast for breakfast.

#382.

After    breakfast,    I    will    get ready  to go  to work.

#383.

I    will  leave  the house  at    9:00  and get

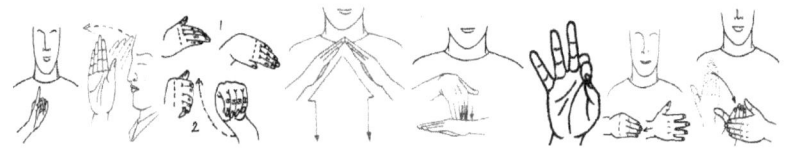

to the office  at    9:30.

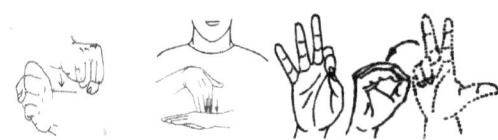

#384.

I  will  probably  go    out    for    lunch.

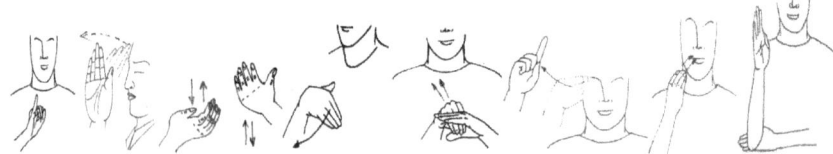

#385.

I   will  finish   working  at           5:30              and

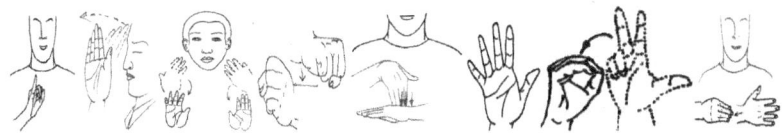

get home by 6 o'clock.

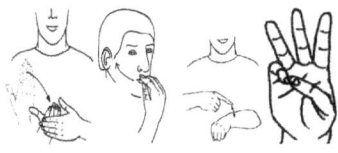

#386.

Are  you  eating  dinner   at   home tomorrow   night ?

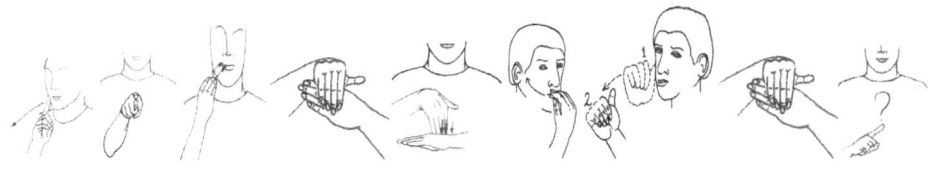

387.

Do        you   think    you    will    go     to   the movies

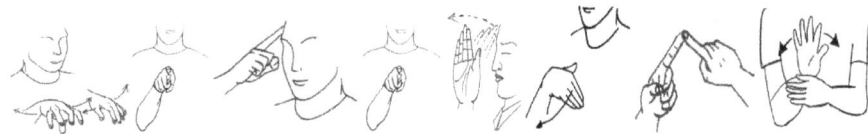

tomorrow    night  ?

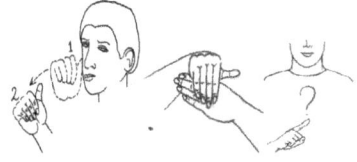

#388.

I    will  probably  stay home  and  watch  television.

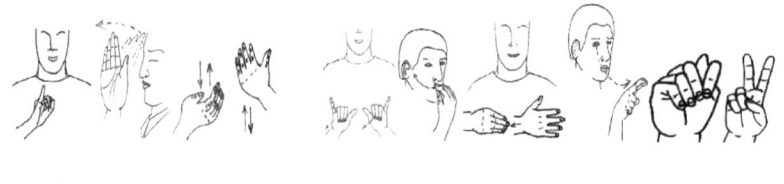

#389.

When  I    become  sleepy,  I    will    probably

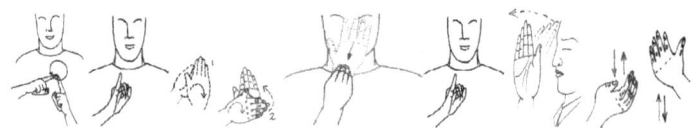

get    ready    for    bed.

#390.

Do  you    think  you    can    go    to    sleep

right away  ?

#391.

How     is     outside   today   ?

#392.

Outside  is      nice.    today.

#393.

What    was outside  yesterday      ?

#394.

Yesterday it    rained    all     day.

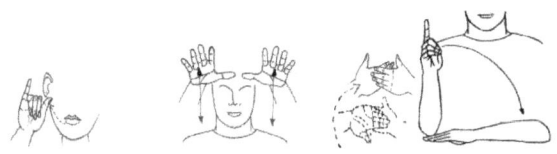

#395.

What will outside be like tomorrow. ?

#396.

Tomorrow snow.

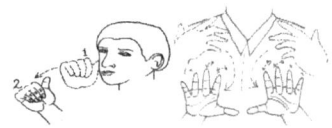

#397.

Very cold today.

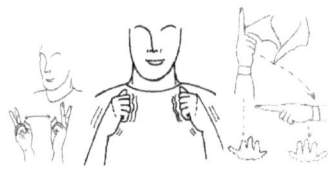

#398.

It's been cloudy all morning.

#399.

Is it   raining   now   ?

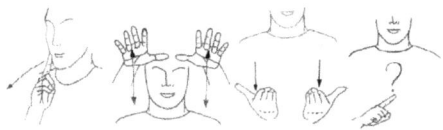

#400.

It'll probably  clear up   this   afternoon.

#401.

The days are becoming      hotter.

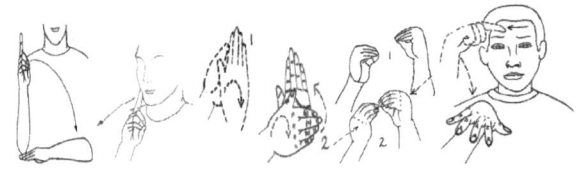

#402.

Today      is  the first  day   of      spring.

#403.

What is the temperature today ?

#404.

This Afternoon about seventy degrees.

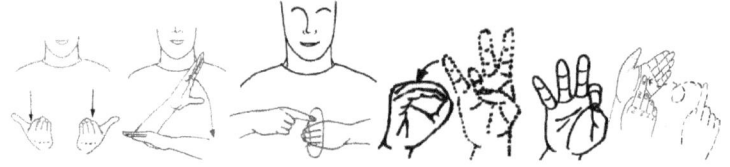

#405.

A cool breeze this evening.

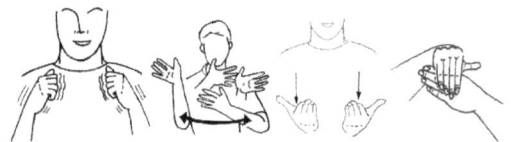

#406.

How are you feeling today ?

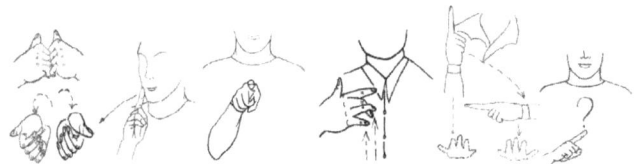

#407.

I    don't    feel    very    nice    this    morning.

#408.

I    was  sick  yesterday, but    I    am    better    today.

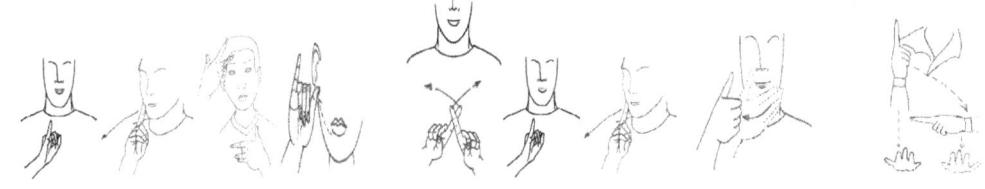

#409.

Your    fever    is    gone   ?

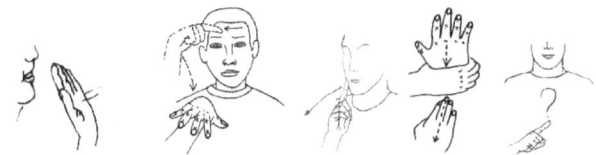

But ,  I    still    have    a    cough.

127

#410.

My     brother     has    a bad    headache.

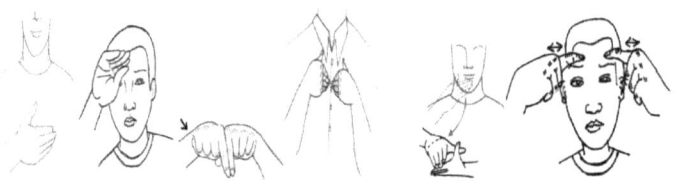

#411.

Which   of   your   arms   is   sore   ?

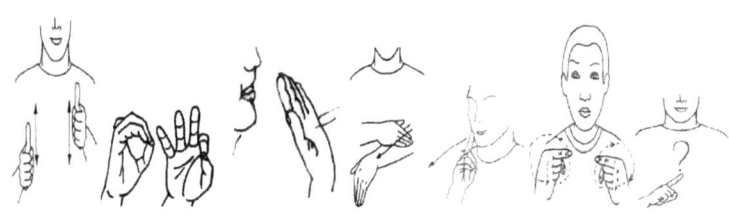

#412.

My right arm hurts It hurts right here

#413.

What's the matter  with   you   ?

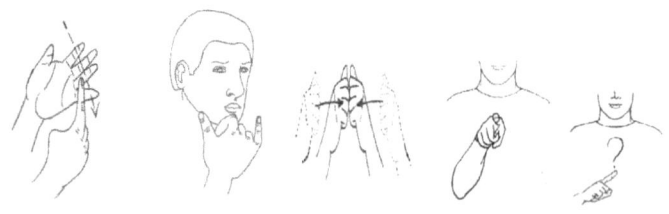

# 414.

I    have    pain    in    my    back.

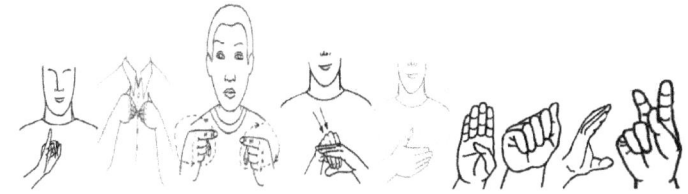

#415.

Which    foot.    hurts    ?    Is it the    left    one    ?

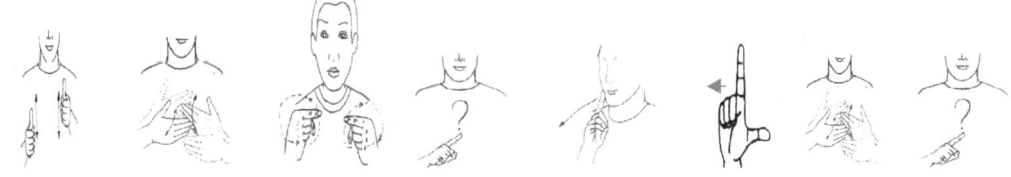

#416.

How    did    you    break    your    leg    ?

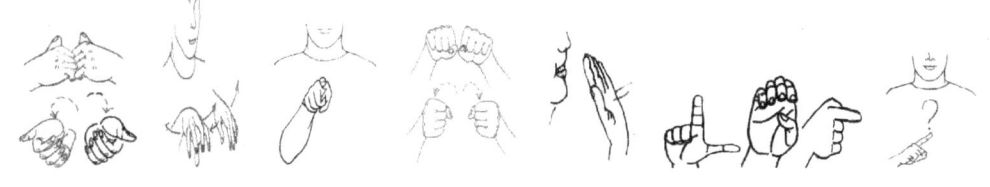

#417.

I    slipped    on the    stairs    I    broke    my    leg.

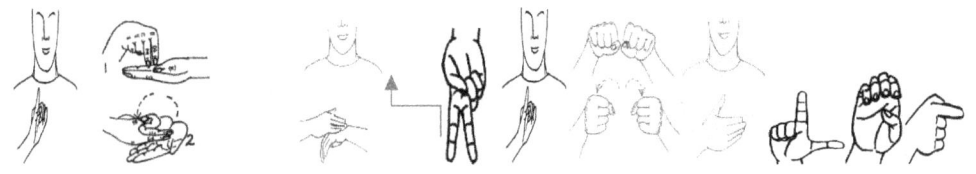

#418.

Your right hand is swollen. Does it. hurt ?

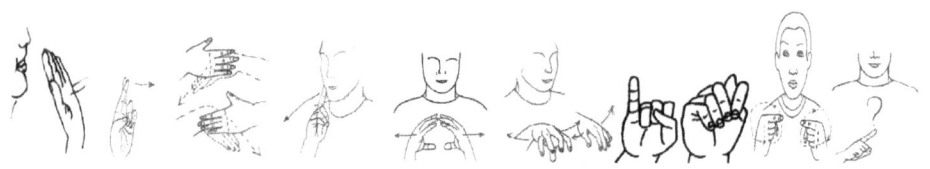

#419.
　　　It　　　is　　bleeding.　You'd better　go　　see

a doctor about that cut.

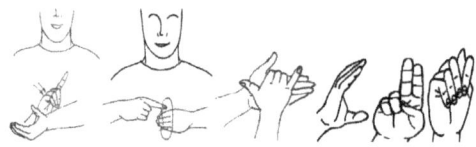

#420.

I hope you'll be well soon.

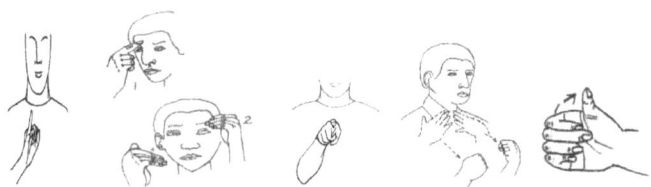

130

#421.

I     get     out of bed     about     7 o'clock every morning.

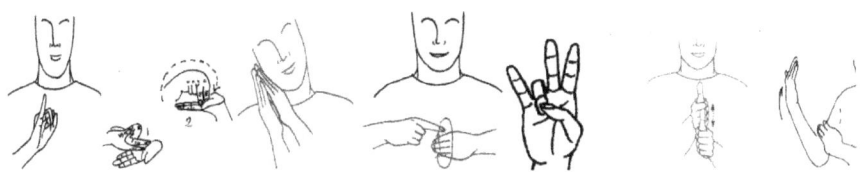

#422.

After     getting up,     I     go     to bathroom     and     take a shower.

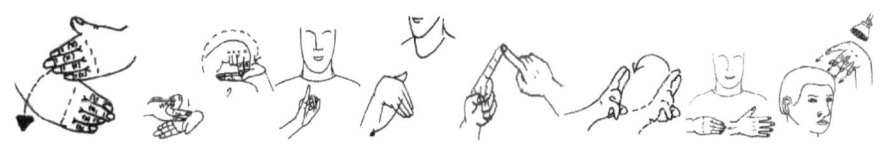

#423.

Then,     I     shave,     brush my teeth, and comb my hair.

#424.

After     brushing     my teeth, I put on my clothes.

  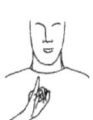 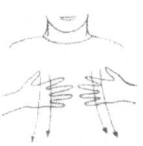

#425.

After   that,   I    go  downstairs  to   the kitchen   to

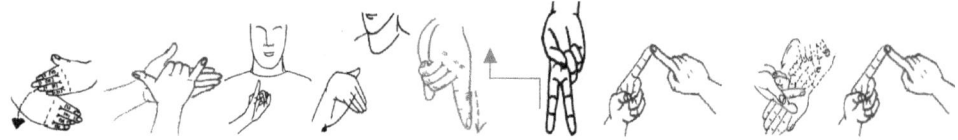

have breakfast.

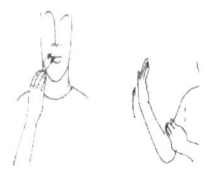

#426.

After  eating  breakfast, I      go back         upstairs.

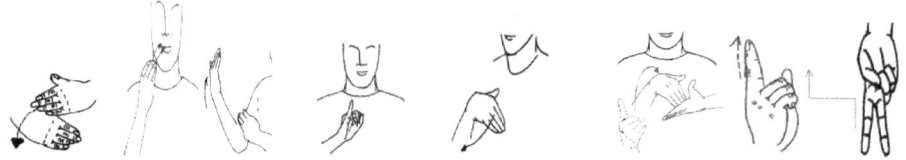

#427.

Then, it's usually  time     to     wake up  my  little.  brother.

#428.

He    can't    dress    himself  yet    because he's too young

#429.

I    wash    his   face   and  hands, then   I   dress   him

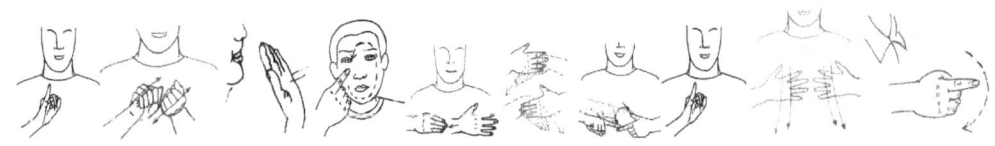

#430.

He     tries    to          button        his

shirt,   but   he    can't   do    it.

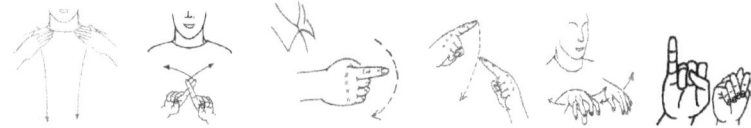

#431.

My     little   brother   bathes     before     he        goes

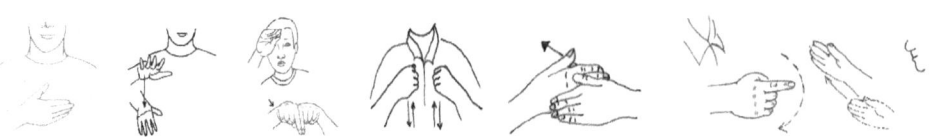

to     bed     at night.

#432.

He         always     forgets     to      wash     behind

his            ears.

#433.

I'm     always     tired    when    I come    home.    from      work.

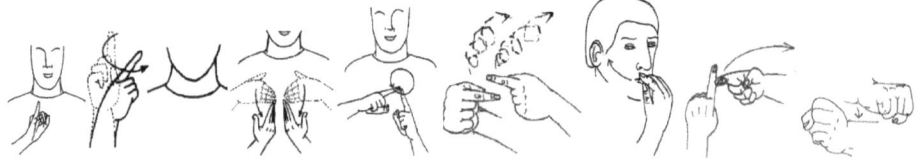

134

#434·

At      bed          time,      I      take off      my clothes

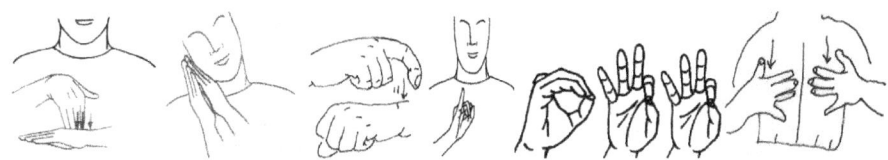

and      put on      my      pajamas.

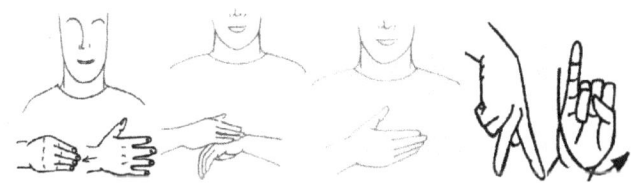

#435·

I  get into   bed    about  11:30,       and   go fast  to sleep

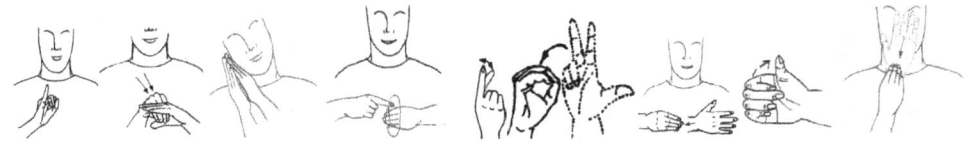

#436.

What     do     you     think    ?       That    right   ?

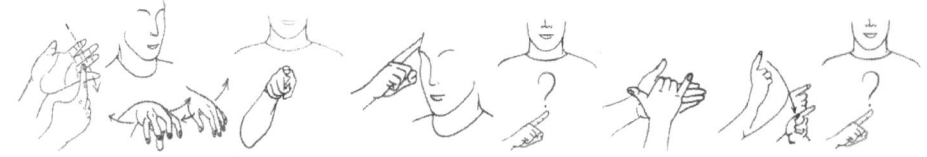

#437.

Certainly   you      are      absolutely   right   about     that.

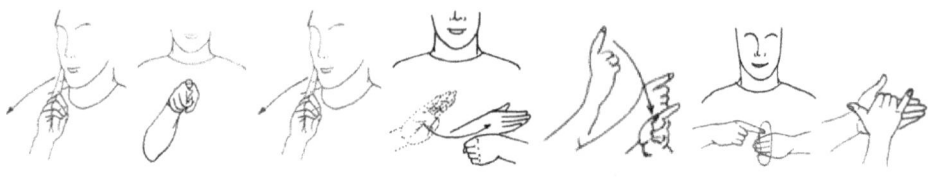

#438.

I     think     you       are   mistaken   about     that.

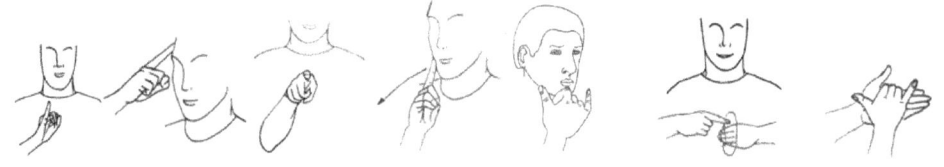

#439.

I     like     hot     weather   best.

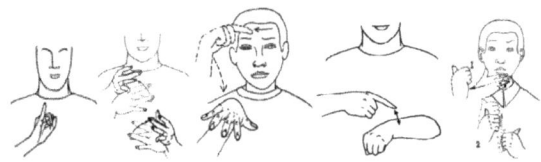

#440.

Personally,  I   prefer   winter weather.

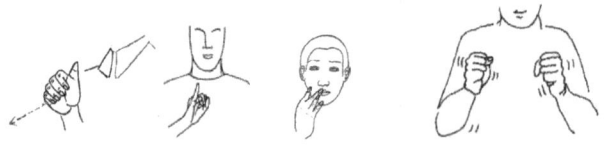

#441.

Do      you      think  it's going to      rain      tomorrow  ?

#442.

I    don't   know   whether   it will rain         or      not

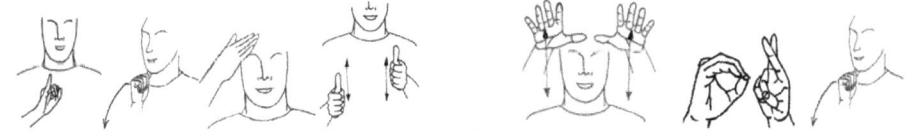

.

#443.

In      my      opinion,    that's  an excellent    idea.

#444.

| Why | is | Mr. | Cooper | so |
|-----|-----|-----|--------|-----|

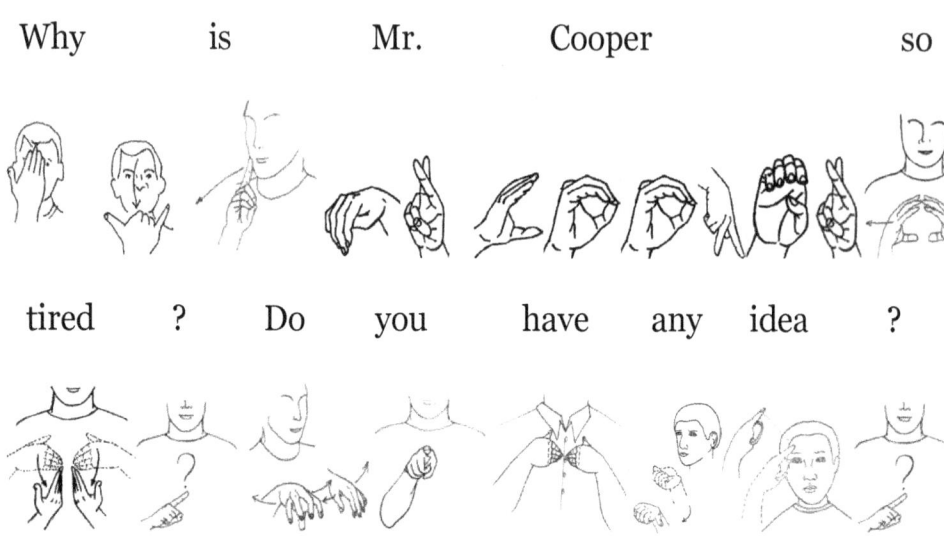

| tired | ? | Do | you | have | any | idea | ? |
|-------|---|-----|-----|------|-----|------|---|

#445.

| He | is | tired | because | he | worked. | hard |
|----|-----|-------|---------|-----|---------|------|

| all | day | today. |
|-----|-----|--------|

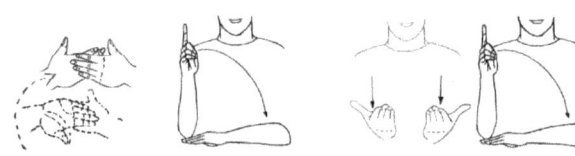

#446.

| What | do | you | think | of | my | children | ? |

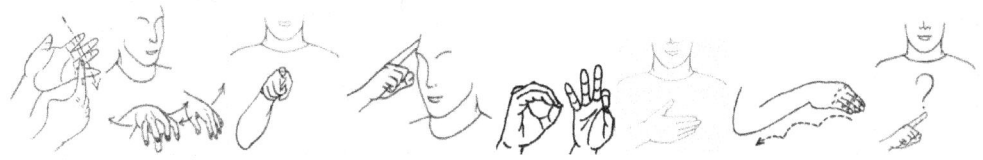

#447.

| I | think | you | have | very | attractive | children. |

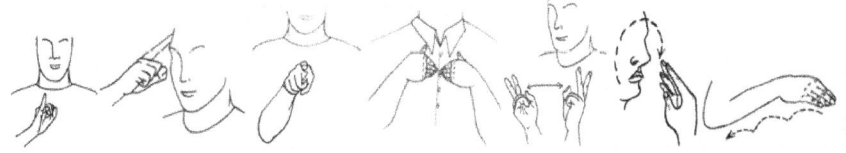

#448.

| Please | tell | me | your | frank | opinion. |

#449.

Do　　　you　　　really　want　　　　to　　　　know

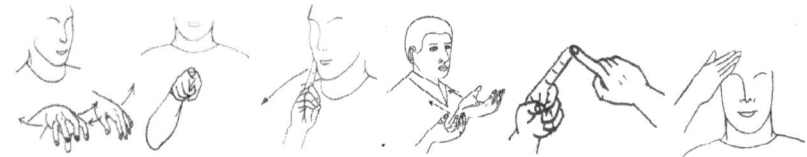

what　　I　　　think　　?

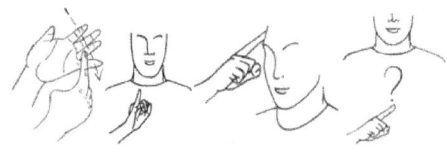

#450.

Of course I　　　want　　　to　　　know　　what　　is

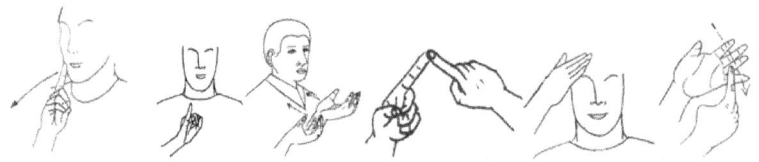

your　　　　opinion

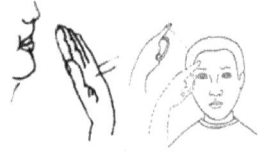

#451.

| What | do | you | plan | to | do | tomorrow | ? |

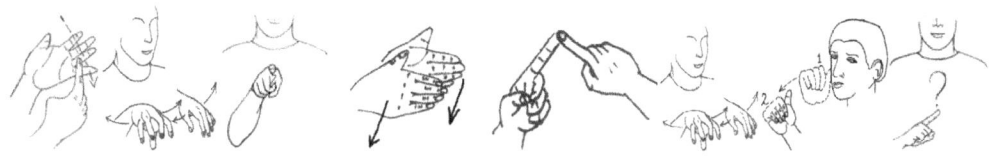

#452.

| I | doubt | that | I'll | do | anything | tomorrow. |

#453.

| Please. | excuse | me | for | a little while. |

| I | want | to | do | some. | thing. |

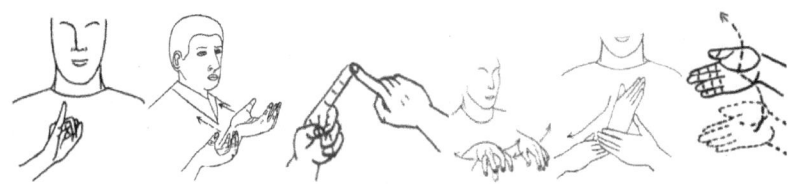

#454.

I imagine I will. do some work

instead of going to the movies.

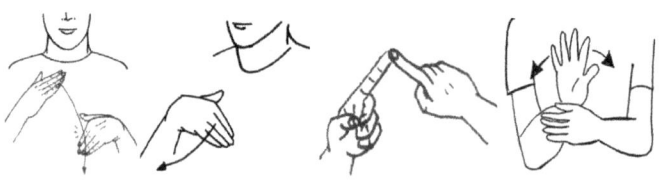

#455.

Will it be convenient for you to explain. your

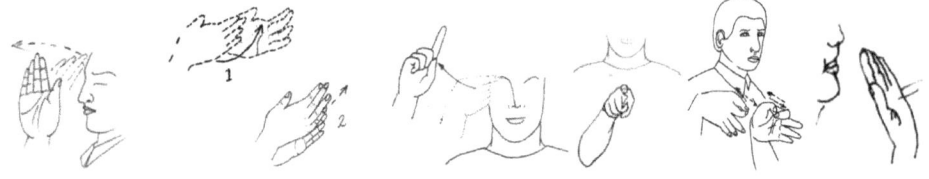

plans to him ?

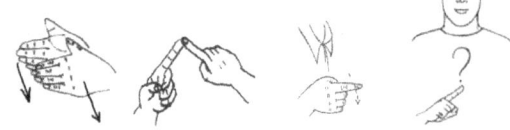

#456.

There's nothing to do because tomorrow

is          a holiday.

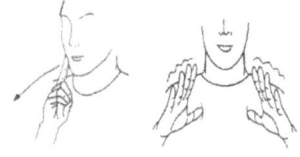

#457.

What        is    your   brother   planning   to

do       tomorrow. ?

143

#458.

He    can't    decide    what    to    do.

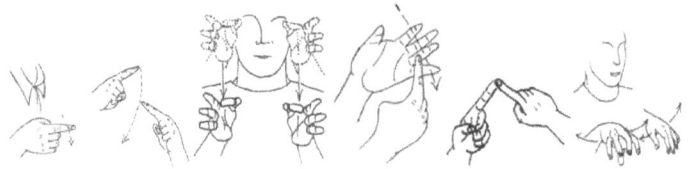

#459.

It's difficult    to    make    a decision    without    knowing

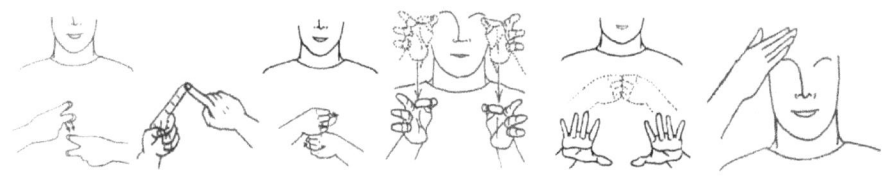

all the                facts.

#460.

We.        are    trying    to        plan        our    future.

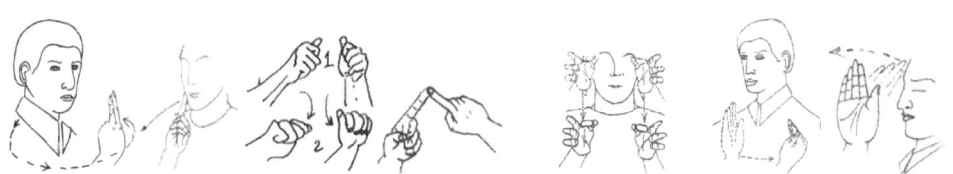

#461.

That      is  a  good     idea.

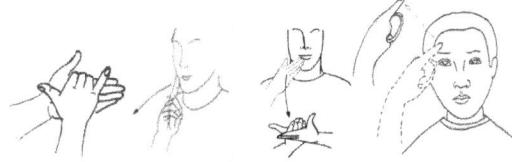

#462.

I    am    hoping     to  stay  a  few   days

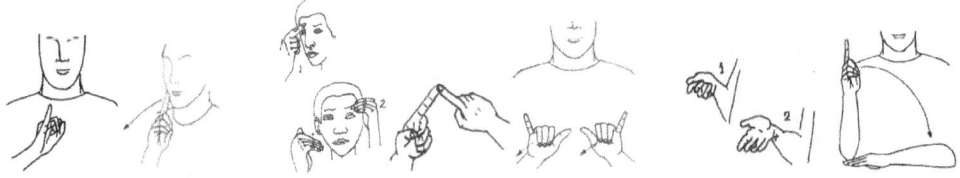

in     the     mountains.

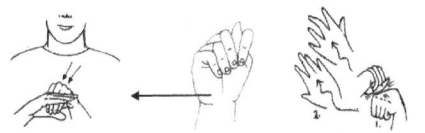

#463.

Would  you      think  about    going      north

this    summer  ?

#464.

If          you          will        go      maybe        I

would          like    to        go      with        you.

#465.

| After | you | think | about it , | let | me | know |
|-------|-----|-------|------------|-----|-----|------|

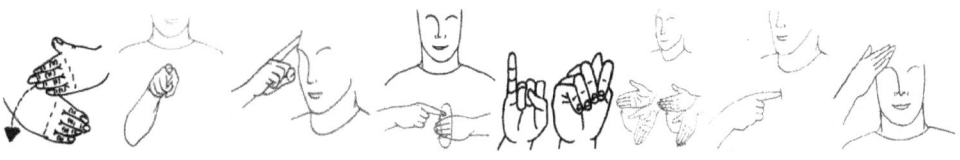

| What | you | decide. |
|------|-----|---------|

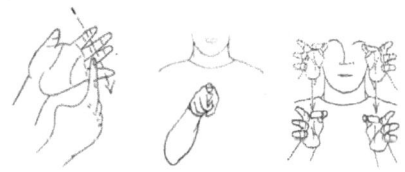

#466.

| I | am | anxious | to | know | your | decision. |
|---|-----|---------|-----|------|------|-----------|

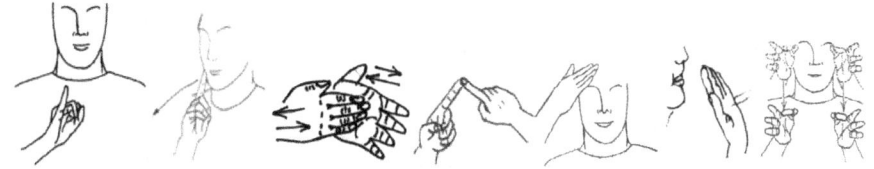

#467.

I    am    confident    you've    made    right

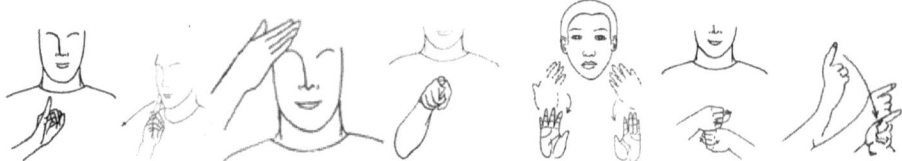

choice.

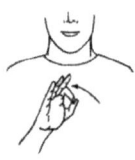

#468.

I    want    to    persuade    you    to    change

your    mind.

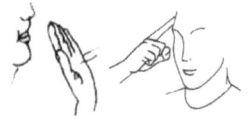

#469.

Will     you    accept.    my    advice    ?

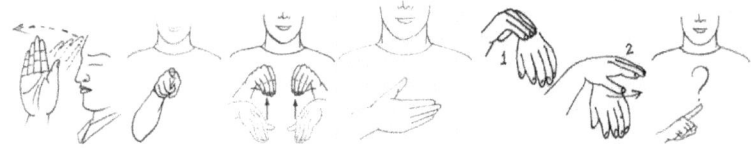

#470.

What    have    you    decided    ?

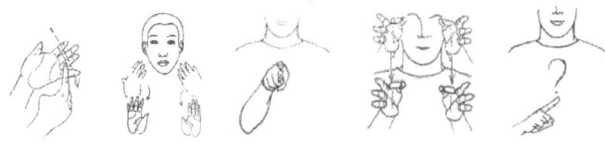

#471.

I    have  definitely  decided    to    go    to    California.

#472.

He      didn't   want     to     say     anything    to

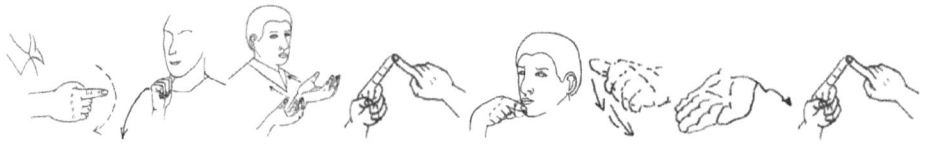

influence    my    decision.

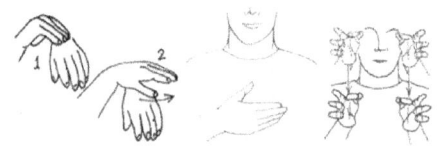

#473.

She      refuses   to   make up   her      mind.

#474.

I    assume   you    have decided against  buying a

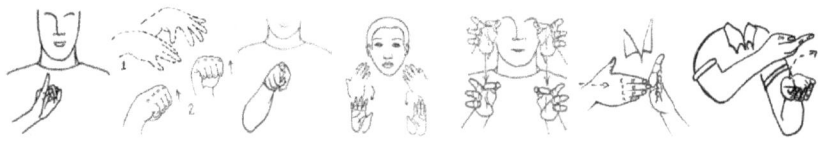

new     car.

#475.

He took long time to decide.

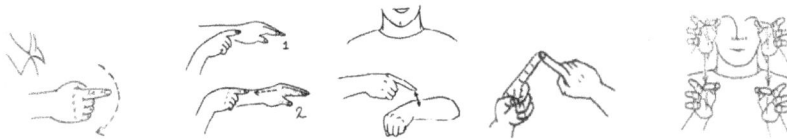

#476.

You can go whenever you wish.

#477.

We are accepting your plan.

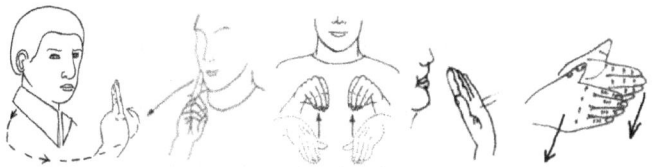

#478.

He    knows    it    is    inconvenient,    but

he    wants    to    go    anyway.

#479.

According    to    Mr.    Green,

this    is    a    complicated    problem.

#480.

She      insists      that  makes   no difference.

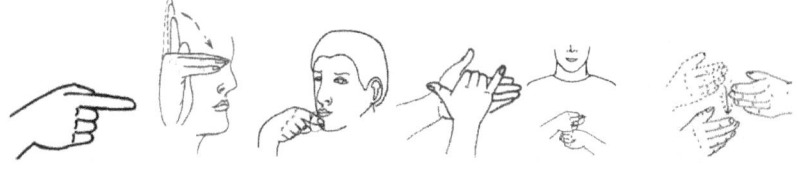

#481.

Are   you.   going   to   any   place   this  year

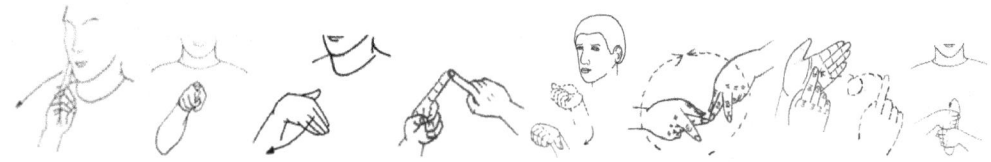

?

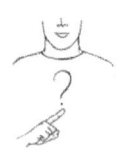

#482.

If     I     have     enough     money,     I     am

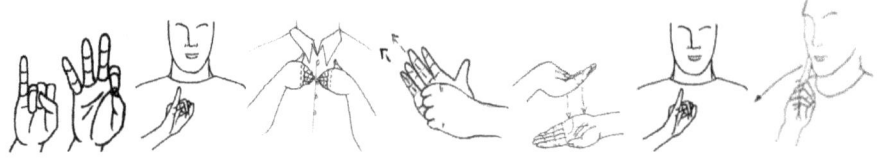

going     to     travel     to     another     country.

#483.

How     are     you     going     ?

Are     you     going     by     boat     ?

#484.

It       is       more    fast      to       go

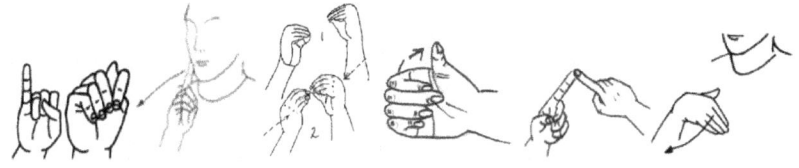

by    plane    than    by     boat.

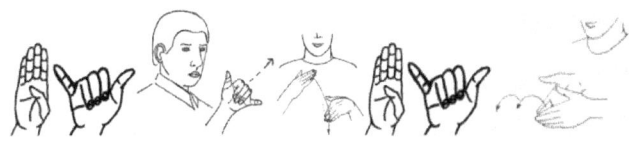

#485.

What    is    the    quickest    way    to

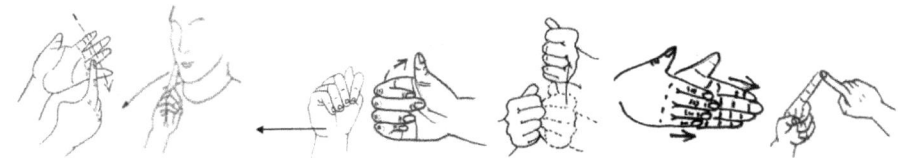

get    there   ?

#486.

Altogether    need.    ten    days    to    make    the

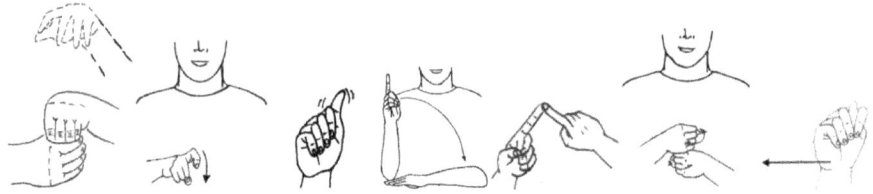

trip.

#487.

I    hope    you    have a good    time

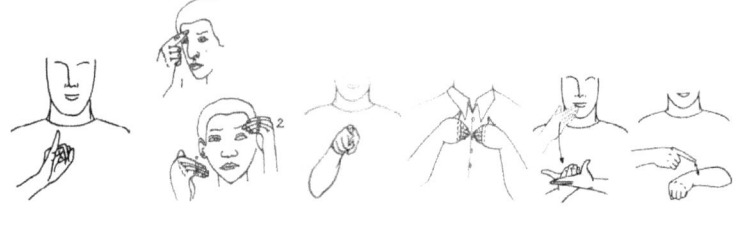

on    your    trip.

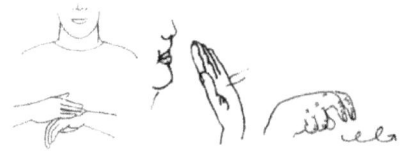

#488.

I        am     leaving    tomorrow, but      haven't

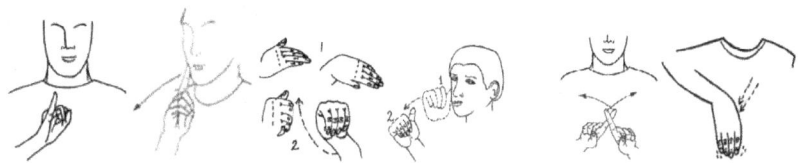

packed  suitcases.

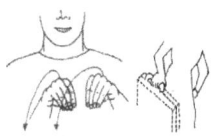

#489.

I        am      going      by         air.

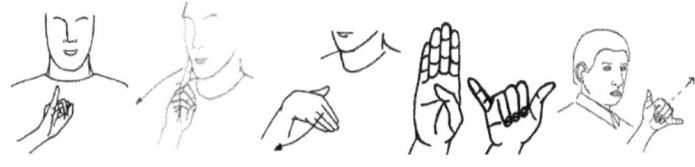

I       like     flying.

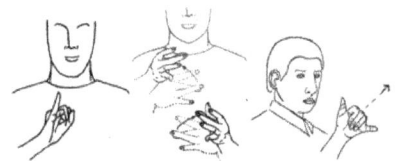

#490.

My    brother    took a trip    to    Mexico.

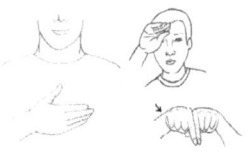 

#491.

It    was    a six    hour    flight.

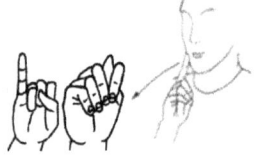 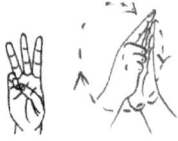 

#492.

How    many    passengers    were    on    the train    ?

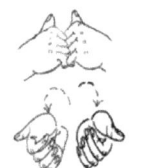  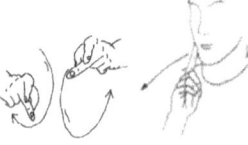 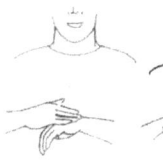 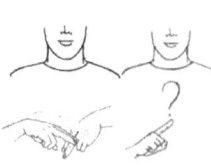

#493.

His    friend    was    injured    in    an airplane    crash

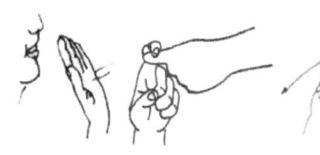 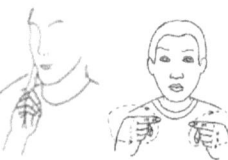 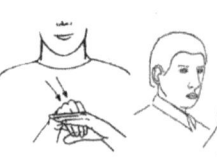 

#494.

Would   you   like   to      go      for

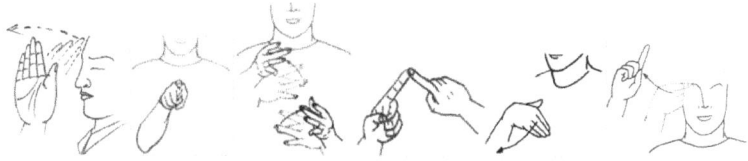

a walk          ?

#495.

Let    us       go       to    the airport.

The plane   landed       ten    minutes ago.

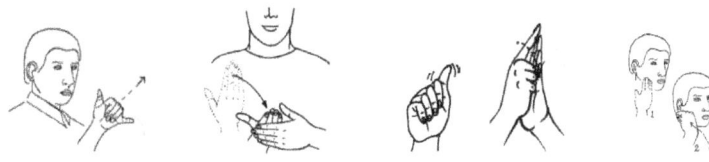

#496.

I am    going shopping because   I   need     to      buy

some      clothes.

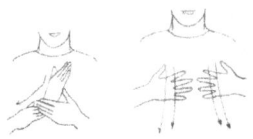

#497.

If       this       shirt   doesn't   fit,       may

I   bring it     back     later    ?

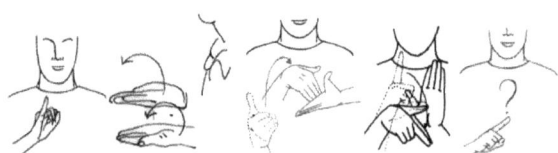

#498.

What    size.     shoes     do     you      have     ?

#499.

That    suit    looks.    very    good    on    you.

#500.

This.        dress    is    made    of                silk,

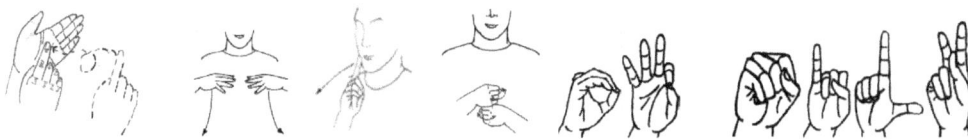

isn't it    ?

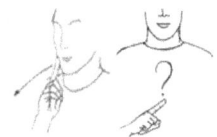

#501.

I    would    like    to    try    on    this    sweater.

#502.

I    am   interested  in.   buying    a new      car.

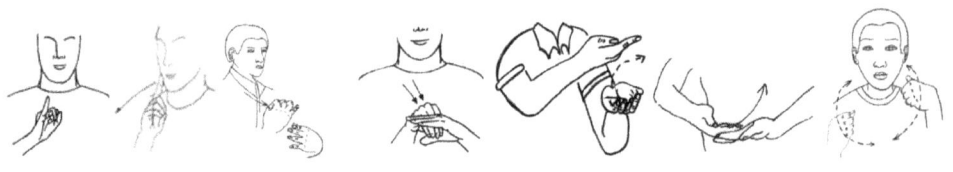

#503.

What  is  the price    of     that     electric

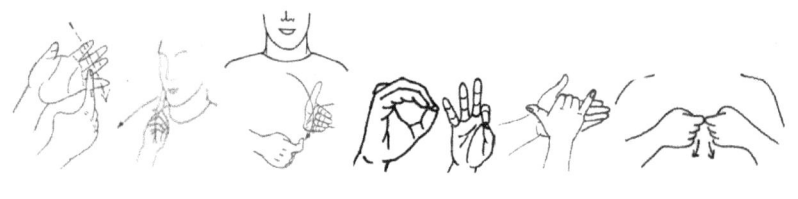

iron           ?

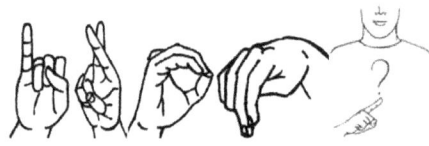

504.

How  much  is    this    rug     ?

#505.

Is　this　toothpaste　on　　　sale

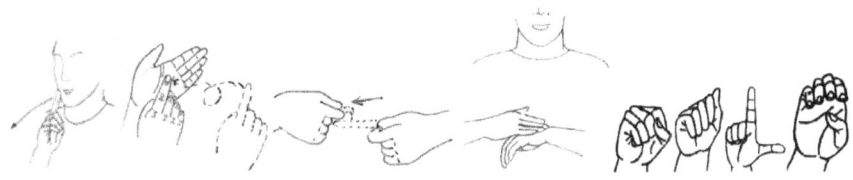

today　　　?

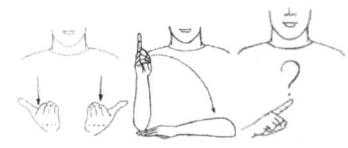

#506.

That　is beautiful　leather , but　　it

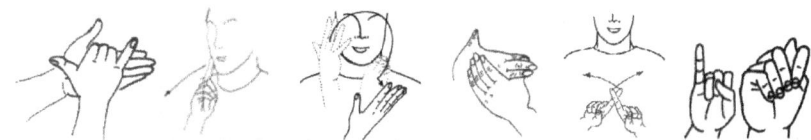

costs　too much.

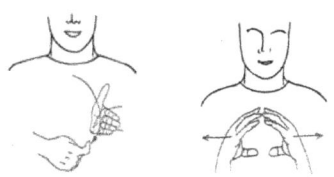

#507.

How   much   I      owe      you      ?

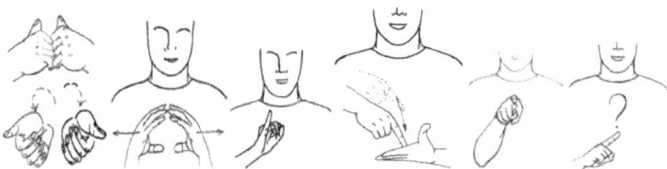

#508.

That will be  eighteen   dollars   and   cents seventy-five.

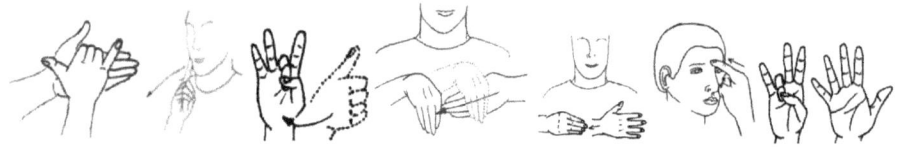

#509.

Do   you   have   change   for   twenty   dollar bill   ?

#510.

The        sales    person    helped    me    find

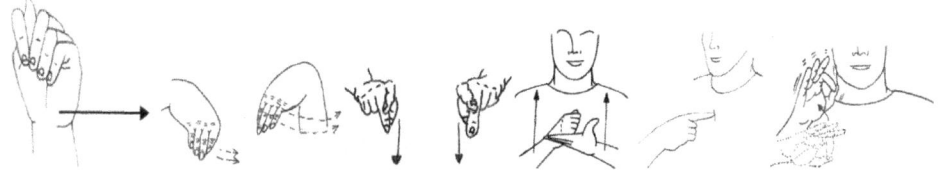

what    I    wanted.

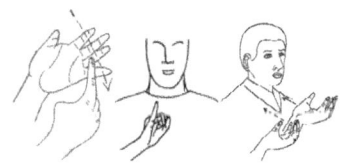

#511.

What   would   you   like   to      eat     ?

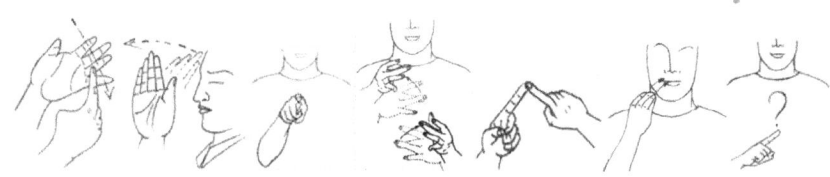

#512.

I'd.   like   a bowl   of   tomato   soup,   please.

#513.

The          waiter       is    in   a hurry

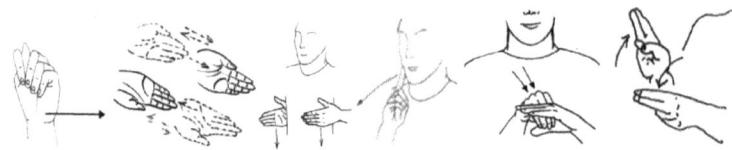

to       take    our   order.

#514,

Which would you rather have ?

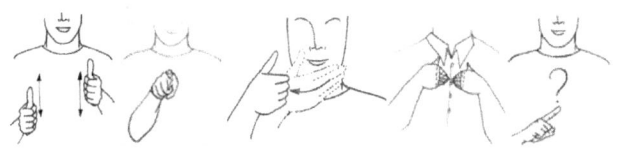

Steak     or    fish   ?

#515.

I      want      my      steak      well-done.

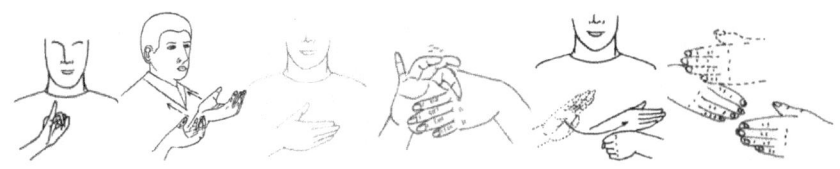

#516.

What  kinds  vegetables      you      have   ?

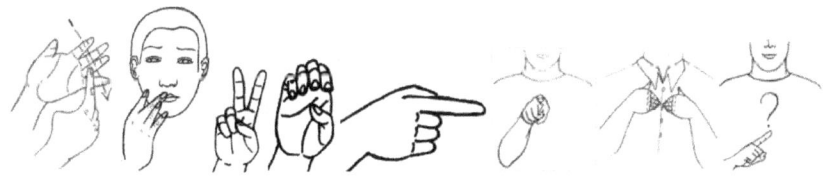

#517.

I      will      have      mashed      potatoes  and    beans.

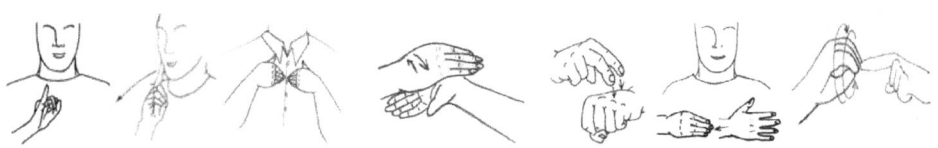

#518.

Would  you  please      pass      the salt   ?

#519.

They.    serve    good.   food    in     this     restaurant.

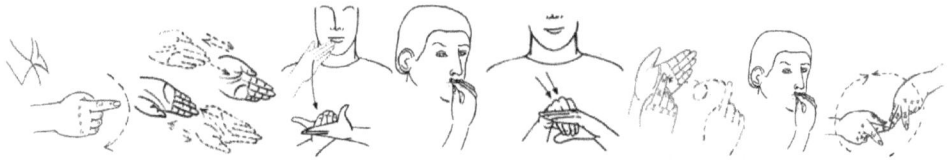

#520.

Are     you     ready     for      your     dessert

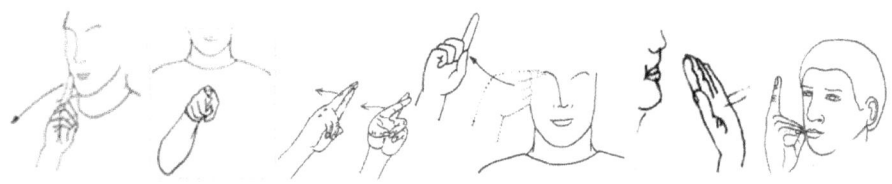

now      ?

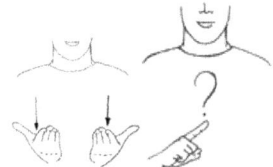

#521.

This           knife           is       dirty      Would

you         bring       me     a clean    one,   please   ?

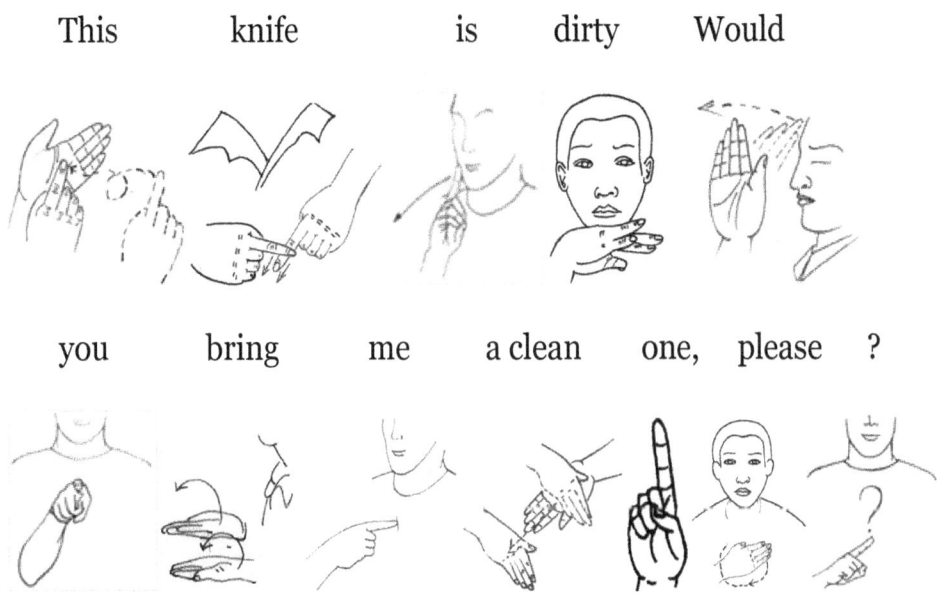

#522.

May   I      have     the check, please   ?

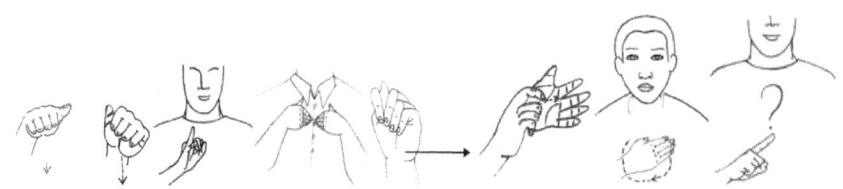

#523.

You    have   your   choice   of   three   flavors

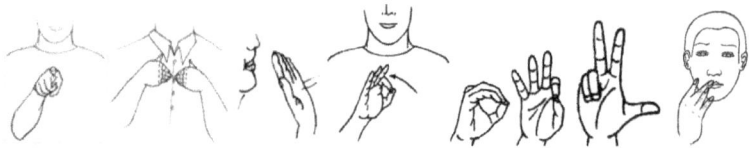

of   ice cream.

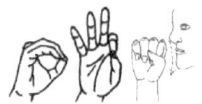

#524.

We    have  vanilla,  chocolate,  and   strawberry.

#525.

We    invited    two guests    to    dinner,

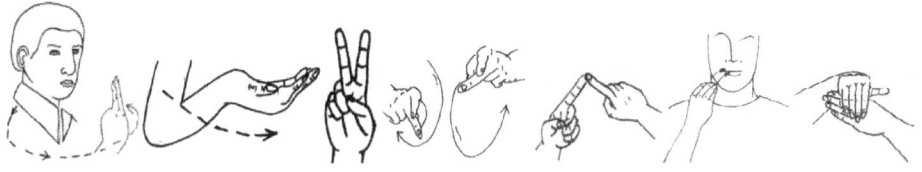

but    they    didn't    come.

#526. How   long    was  the movie   ?

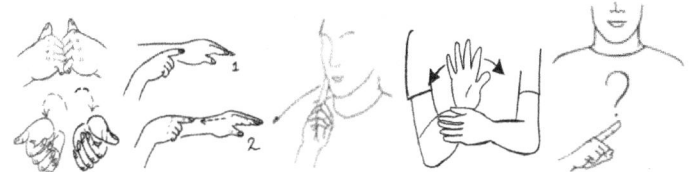

#527.

The feature started at 9 o'clock

and ended at 11:30.

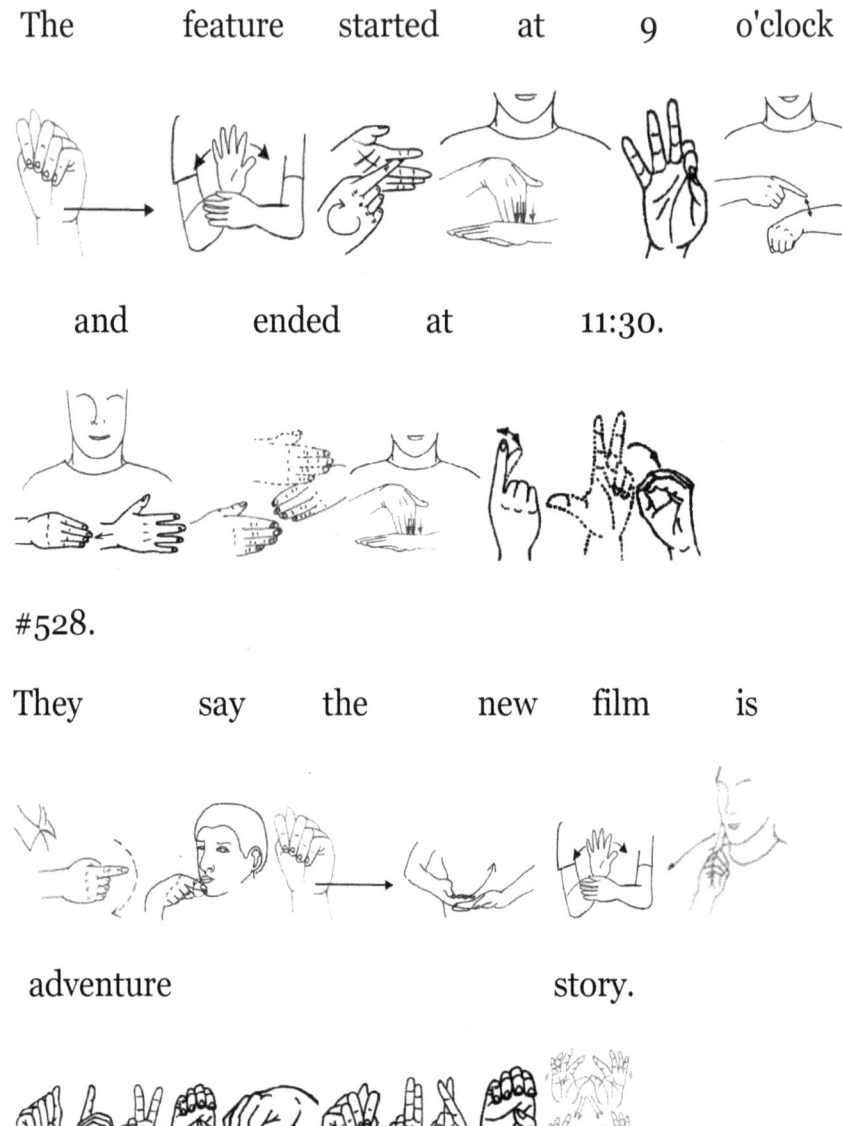

#528.

They say the new film is

adventure story.

#529.

A    group    of    us    went    out    to    the

theater             last       night.

#530.

The    new    play    was    good    every

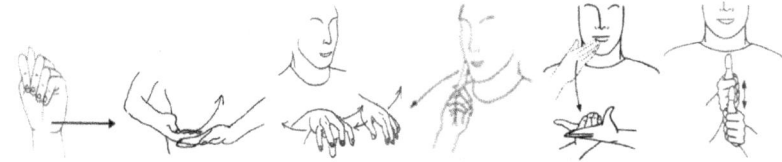

body    enjoyed    it.

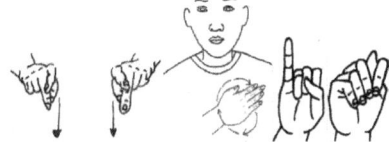

#531.

By the time      we     got there,     play  had already  begun.

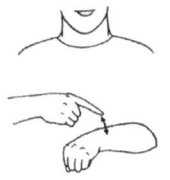 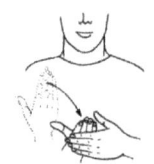  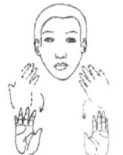 

#532.

The    usher showed     us    to     our    seats.

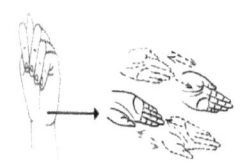 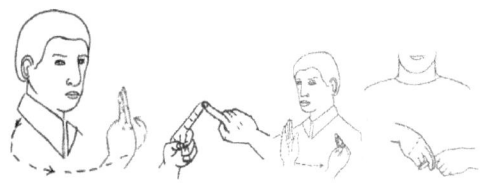

#533.

The     cast    of    the   play included   a   famous

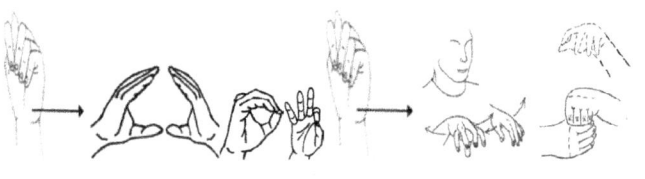 

actor.

#534.

After    the    play    was    over,    we    all

wanted    to    get something    to eat.

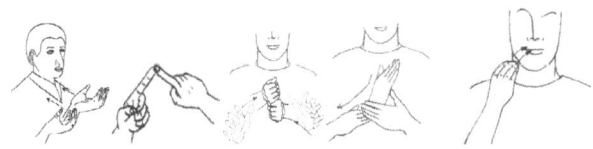

#535.

There    was    a big    crowd    and    we

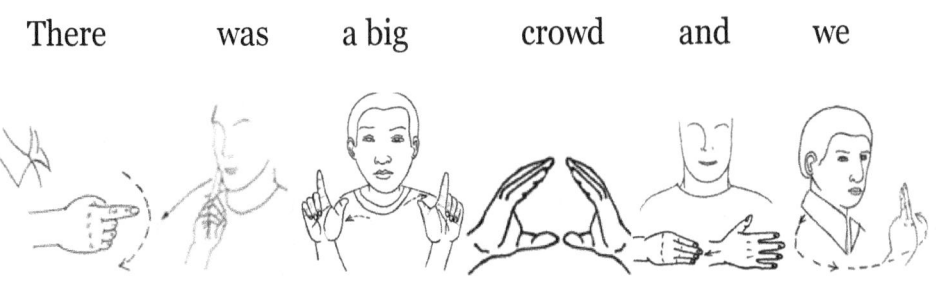

had    difficult    time    getting    a taxi.

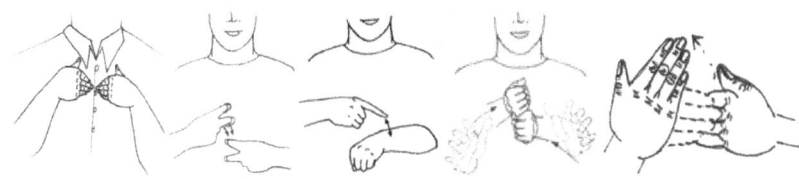

175

#536.

The            restaurant        filled,        so            we

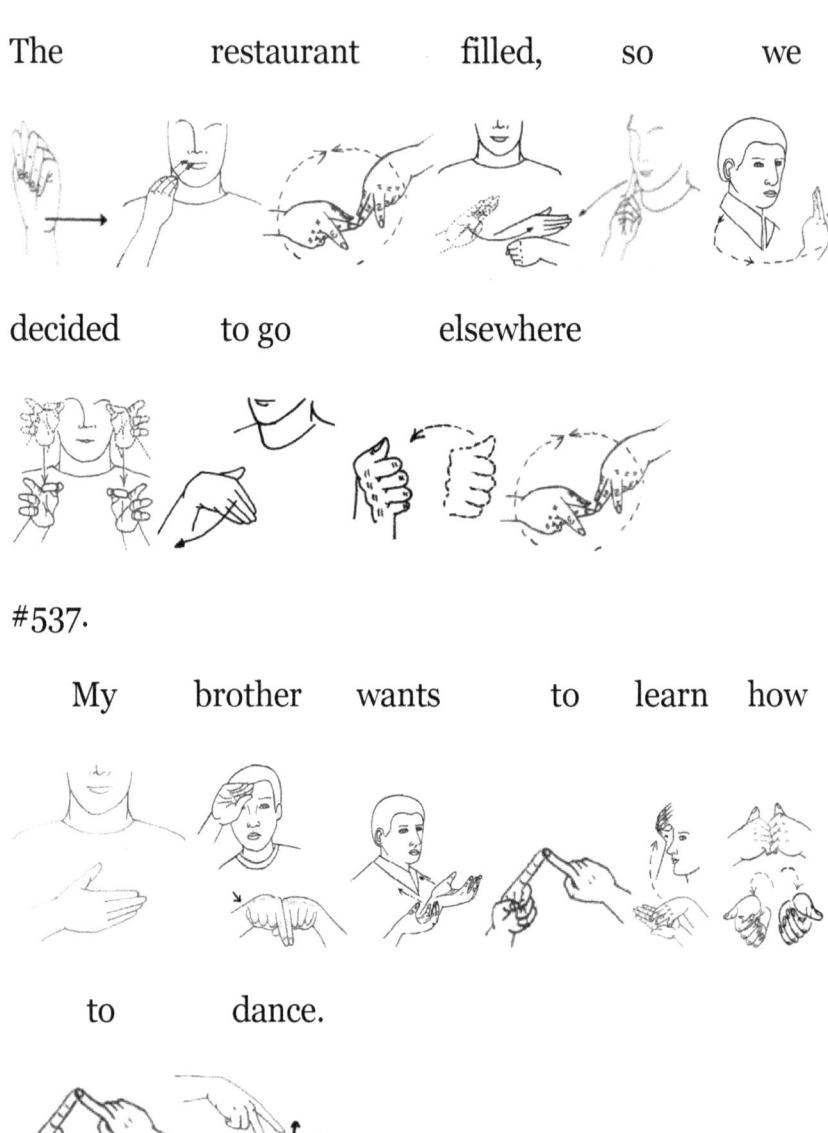

decided        to go          elsewhere

#537.

My        brother        wants        to        learn        how

to            dance.

#538.

We        don't        go    dancing    very      often.

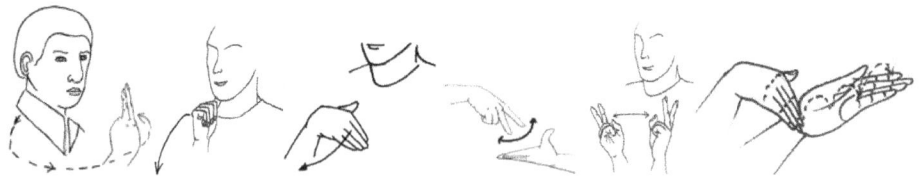

#539.

Which  would   you       rather     do;        go

dancing      or       go    to   a    play    ?

#540.

| I | am | not | accustomed | to |
|---|----|----|-----------|----|

| going | out | after | dark. |
|-------|-----|-------|-------|

#541.

| I'd | like | to | make | plan | to |
|-----|------|----|------|------|----|

| see | Mr. | Cooper. |
|-----|-----|---------|

#542.

Would     you     like          to          arrange

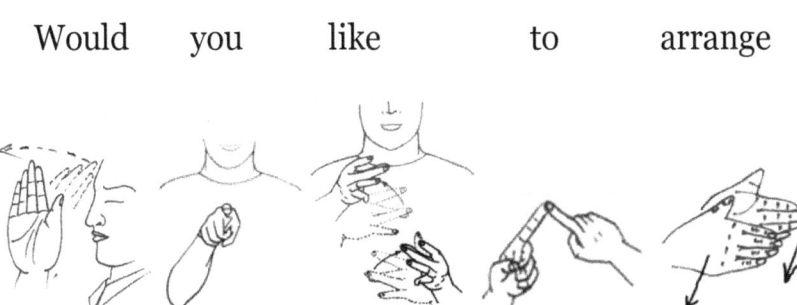

for     a personal     interview ?

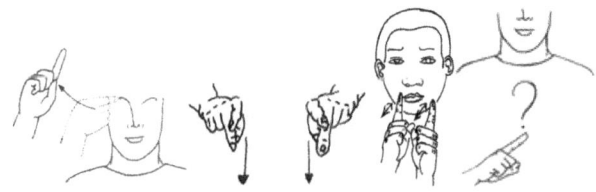

#543.

Your     meeting          will          be          next

Thursday          at          time          10

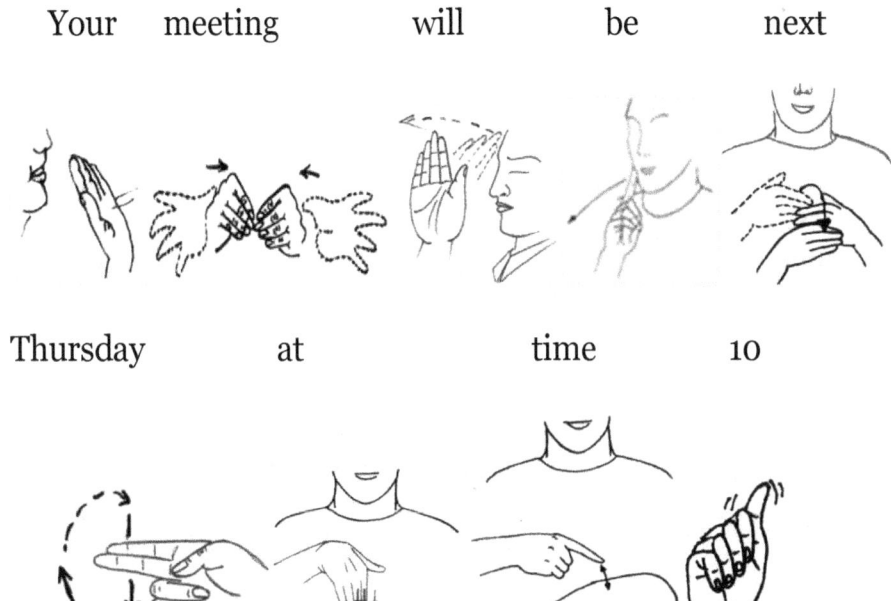

#544.

I       can       come       any       day       except       Thursday.

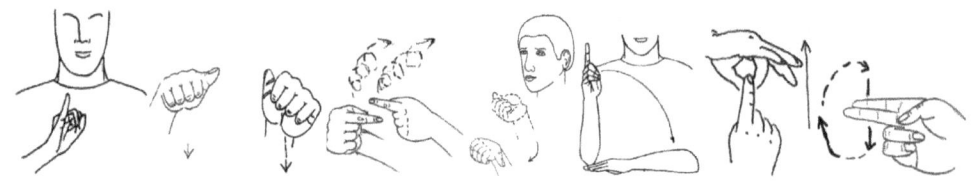

#545.

He       wants       to       change       his       meeting

from    . Monday       to       Wednesday.

#546.

She did not call to cancel

her meeting.

#547.

I'm going to call the employment

agency for a job.

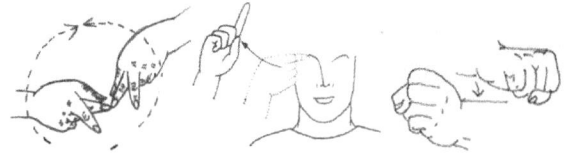

#548.

Please    fill in    this    application.

#549.

Are    you    looking    for    a permanent    position

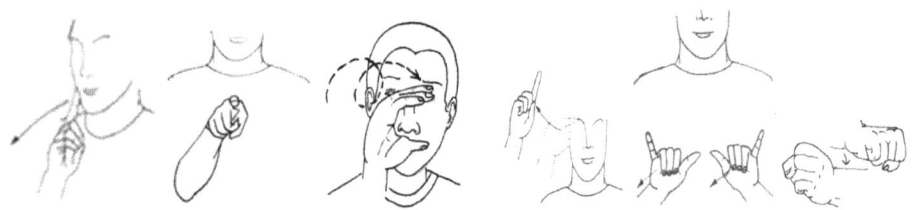

?

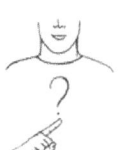

#550.

I        am        calling        plumber

to    come    this    afternoon.

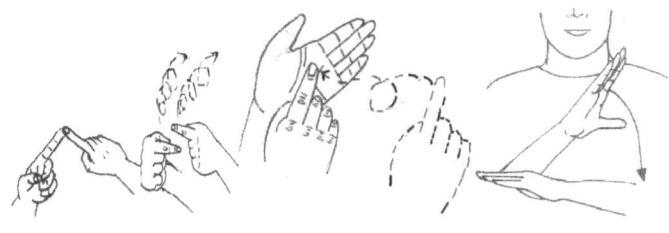

#551.

I  couldn't  keep   meeting  because  I  was sick.

#552.

I      am      a new   employee.

I      was.     hired    yesterday.

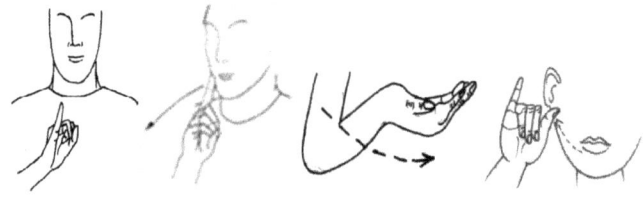

#553.

Please    call   before   you     come,

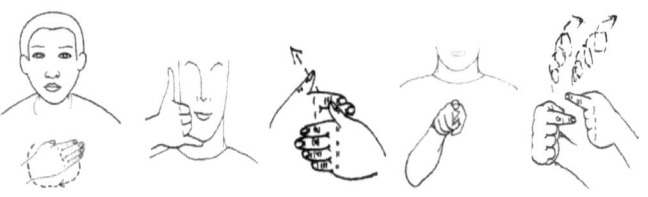

we      might     not   be home.

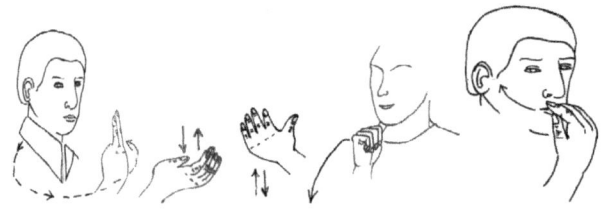

#554.

Let    us    make    time    meet    go

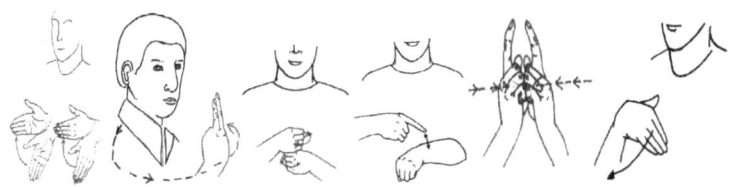

shopping  next    Thursday.

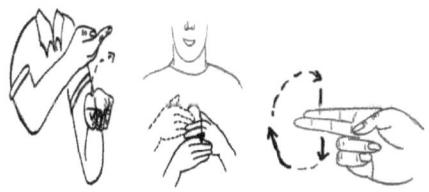

#555.

Will      you              lock      the door  when    leaving      ?

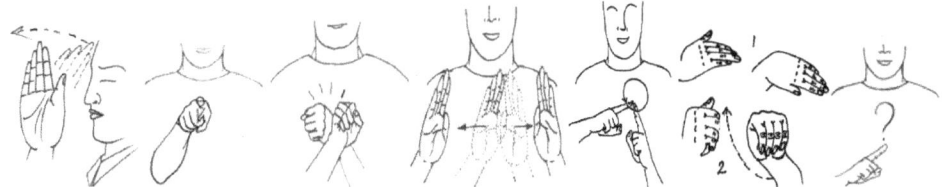

#556.

I     went    to      see     my      doctor

for       a check-up   yesterday.

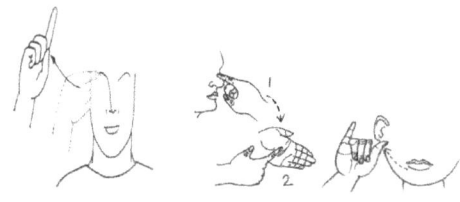

#557.

The doctor  discovered  I'm  a little     overweight.

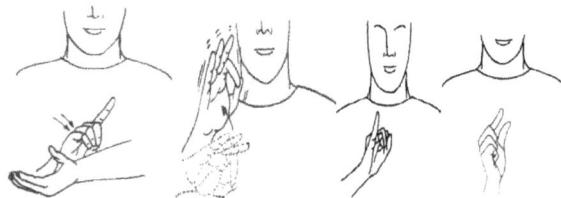

#558.

He         gave        me        chest       X-ray

and      took      my      blood    pressure.

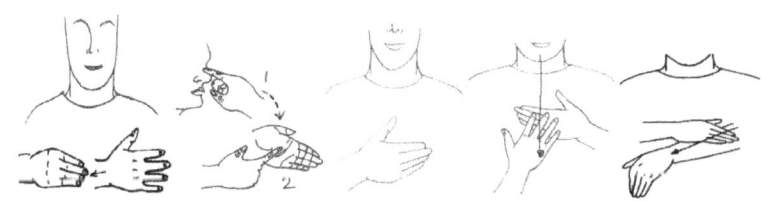

#559.

He    told    me   take pills every  four  hours.

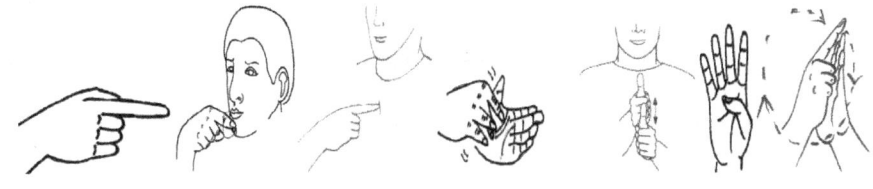

#560.

Do.   you   think the   patient   can  be cured  ?

#561.

They    operated    on    him    last    night.

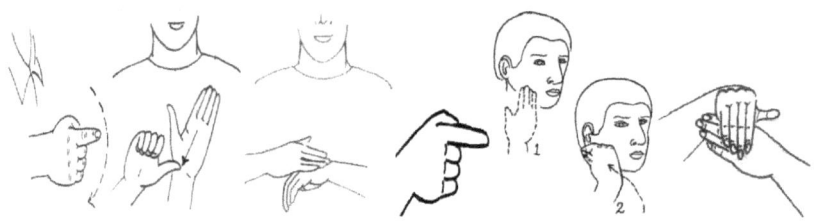

#562.

He    needed a blood    transfusion.

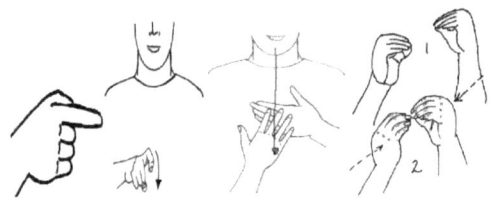

#563.

My uncle    had    a heart    attack    last    year.

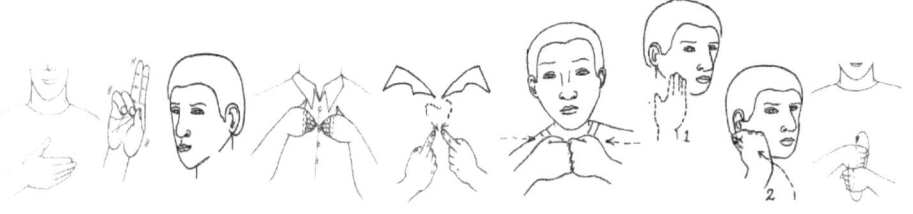

#564.

They  needed   to call  a heart    specialist.

#565.

What    did    the doctor    say  ?

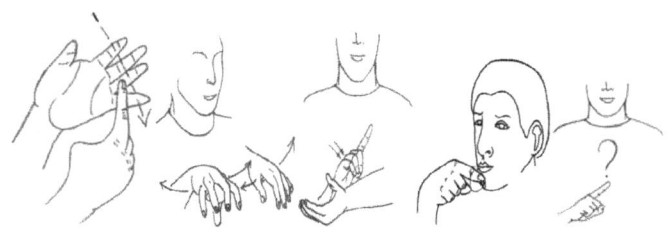

#566.

The doctor advised.        me    to     get    plenty

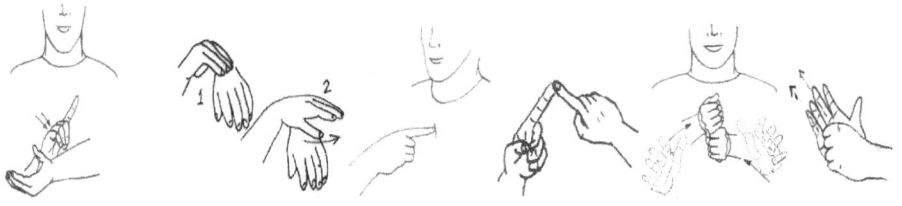

of exercise.

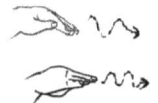

#567.

The doctor said     I       look      pale.

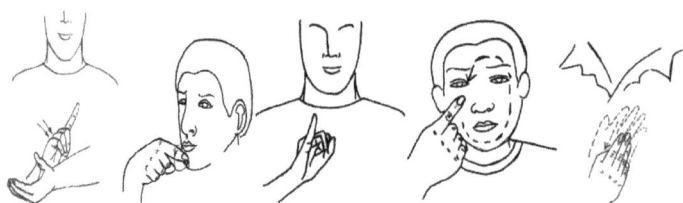

#568.

If      I       want      to be   healthy

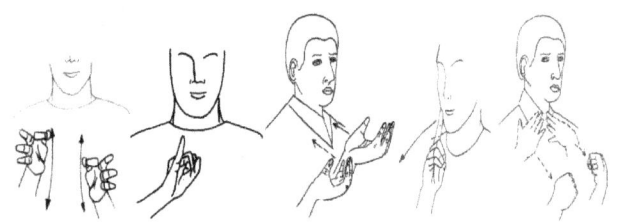

I       need     stop          cigarettes.

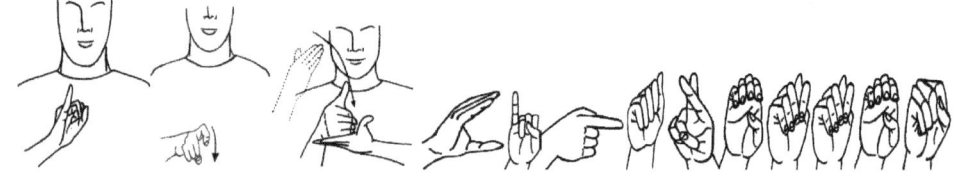

#569.

The physician said     smoking     is     harmful to   my    health.

#570.

It's     mosquito bite. There's nothing    to worry    about.

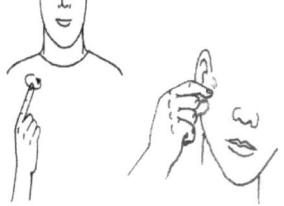 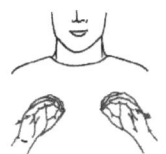 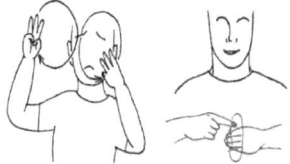

#571.

Telephone   wants  you.

#572.

What     dial to        phone    operator?

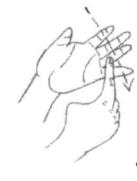  

#573.

I     want    to make   a long distance  call.

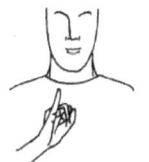  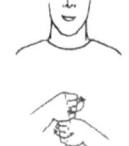  

191

#574.

Pick up    the receiver    and    deposit  a coin    in the slot.

#575.

I    tried    to call    Mr.    Cooper,

but    the line    was busy.

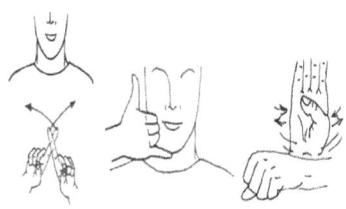

#576.

You.   must    wrong    called.

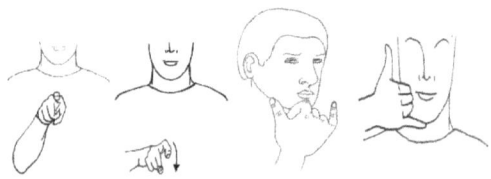

#577.

I   dialed   the right,   but   nobody   answered.

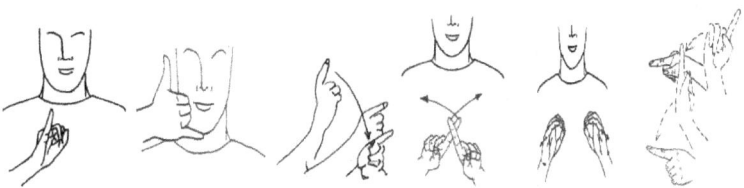

#578.

Telephone is ringing.   Would   you

answer it,   please.   ?

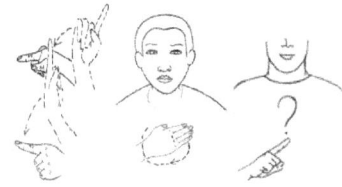

#579.

Would   you.   like.   to   leave   a message ?

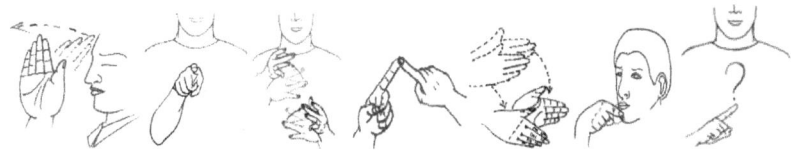

#580.

Who is this ?    I    don't  recognize  your    voice.

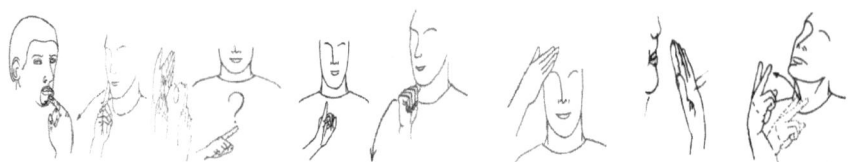

#581.

Would.   you    please         tell      Mr.

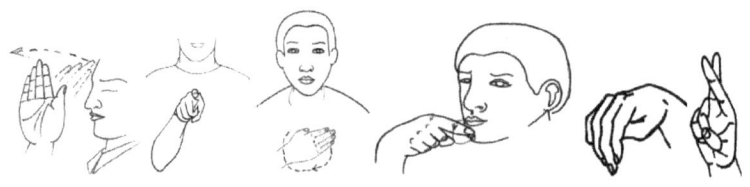

Cooper              I    called    ?

#582.

Is    this    5    4    0    9    3    ?

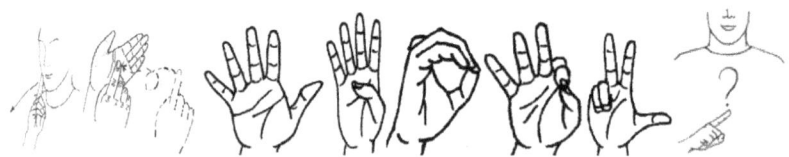

#583.

I   must       hang up   now.

#584.

I  can't       hear     you.

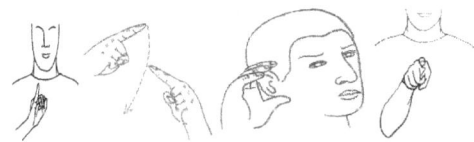

#585.

Would     you       mind.     calling    back   tomorrow. ?

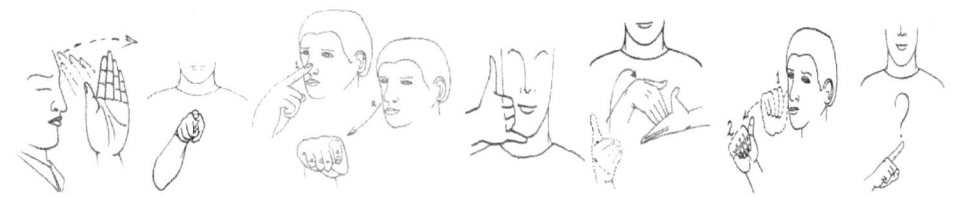

#586.

How    long    since. you've  heard  from your  uncle    ?

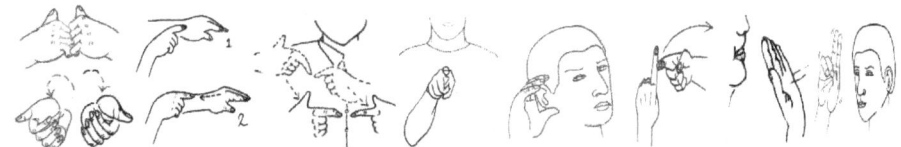

#587.

When    was    the last    time    he    wrote    you?

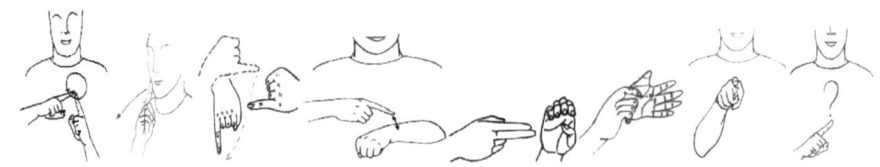

#588.

I    can't    recall    how    long    it's been.

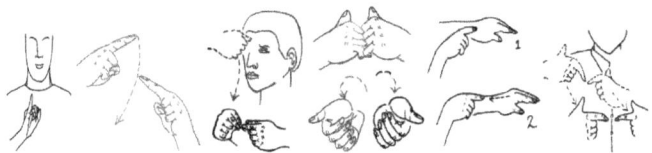

#589.

I'm    always disappointed when I    don't get    any    mail.

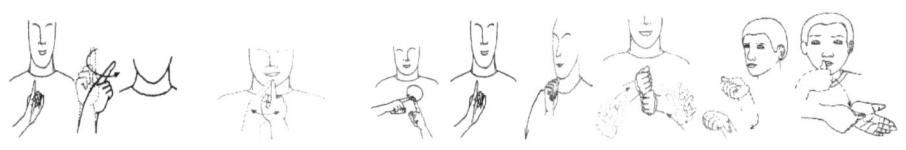

#590.

I    feel    guilty    because I    haven't    written    her.

#591.

What time   is the mail delivered   on   Saturday  ?

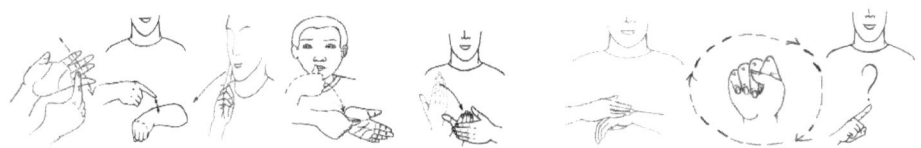

#592.

The   postman   always  comes at   3   o'clock.

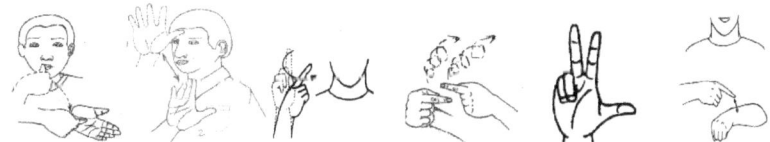

#593.

I   wrote   to   my   uncle   last.   night.

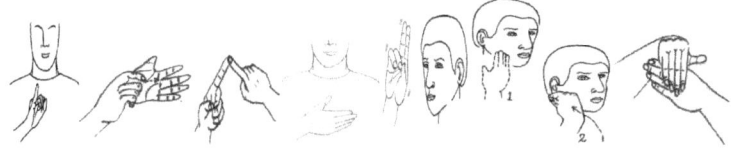

#594.

I  enclosed  some photographs in   my.   letter.

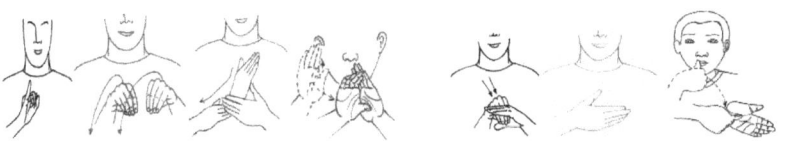

#595.

I didn't know whether to send letter airmail or not.

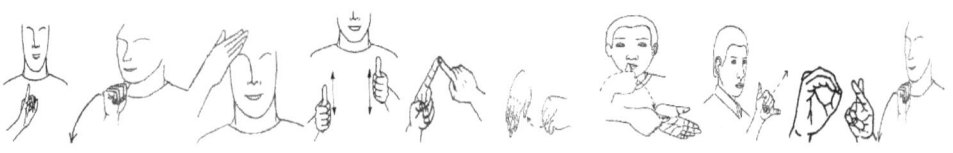

#596.

How long for. a letter to get to California ?

#597.

Don't forget. to put. on stamps before you mail it.

#598.

He went to the post office to mail a letter.

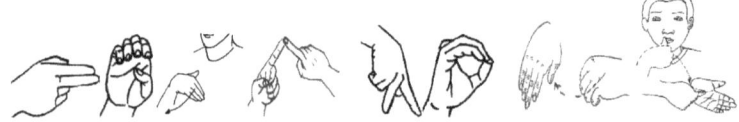

# 599.

I    dropped.    the letter    in    mail.        box.

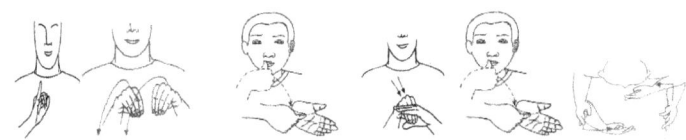

#600.

Did        you        write    and        sign    the letter    ?

#601.

A strange thing    happened        to    me    this    morning.

#602.

I was    crossing the    street.    and was almost    hit        by a        car.

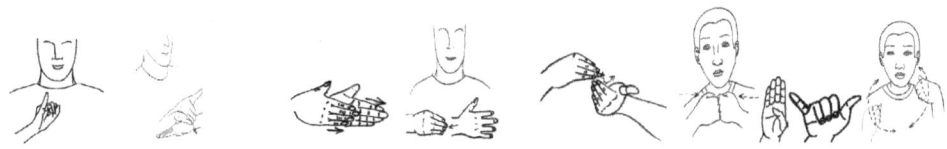

#603.

I    jumped back  in    time to   not be   hit.

#604.

It was a   terrible   experience, and   I    won't     forget it.

#605.

Yesterday   was such a beautiful day we     decided   to    go for a

drive.

#606.

We    prepared a    picnic               lunch    by   the river.

#607.

After a while,   we   found a   shady   place   under   some

  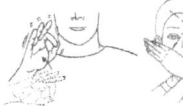  

trees.

#608.

On the   way home, we   had a   flat   tire.

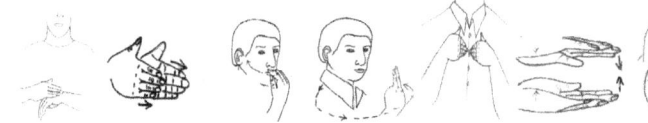

#609.

After   dark   we   arrived  home, and   we were all   tired.

#610.

I wish you would explain more about your trip.

#611.

Did I tell you about my travel experience. ?

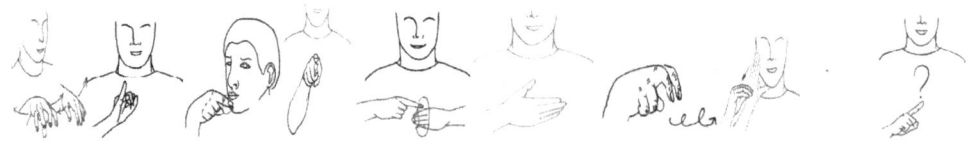

#612.

We used to have a lot of fun when we were that age.

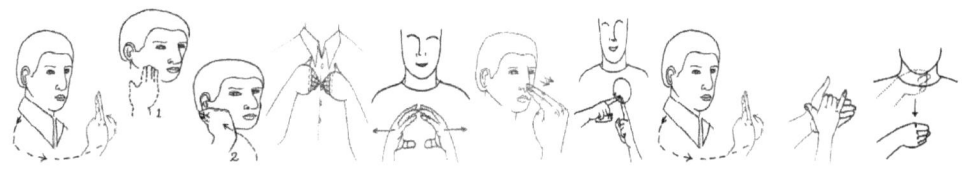

#613.

I can't recall exactly what happened.

#614.

I  never  realized  some. day  I  would

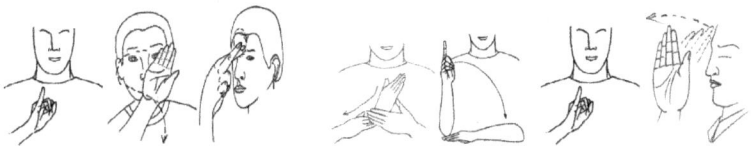

be  living in  New York.

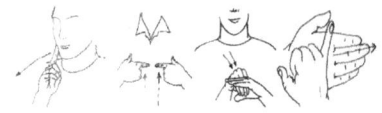

#615.

We  never  imagined  John  would  become a doctor.

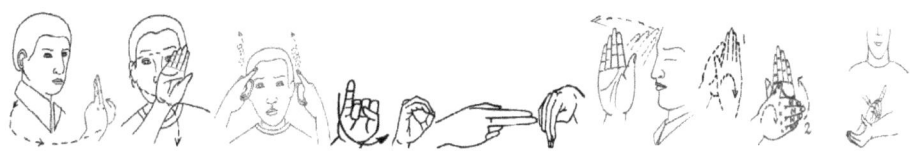

#616.

We're  looking  for  a house  to  rent  for.  the summer.

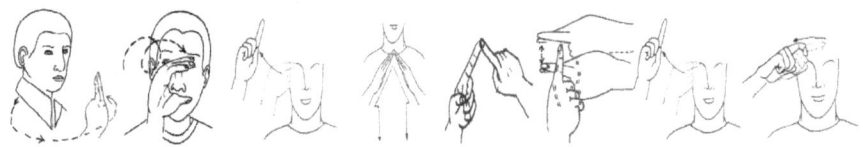

#617.

Are  you  trying to  find  a  furniture  house ?

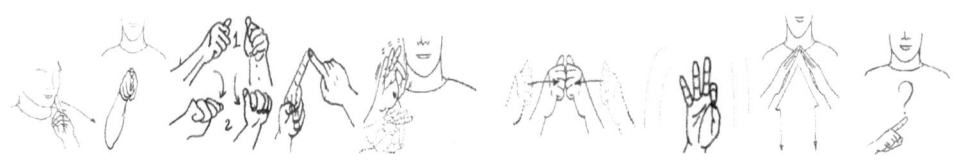

#618.

This  split-level  house  is  for  rent.

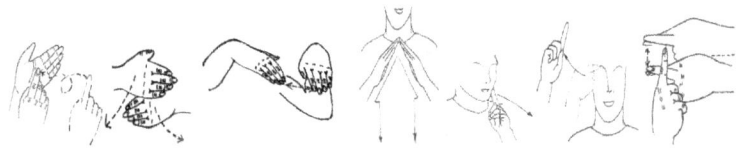

It  is  a bargain.

#619.

That  house is  for  sale.

#620.

We   have   a few.   kitchen  things   and a dining room  set.

#621.

This   is an   interesting  floor  plan. Please  show  me the basement.

#622.

The front          steps          need   to be fixed.

#623.

We    need    to   get  a bed   and   a dresser for the bedroom.

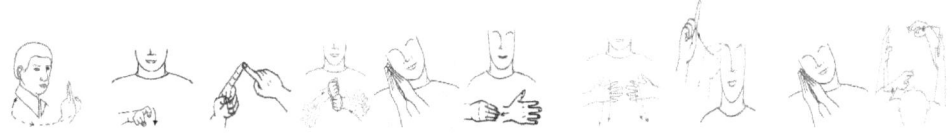

#624.

Does the back       door  have   a lock        ?

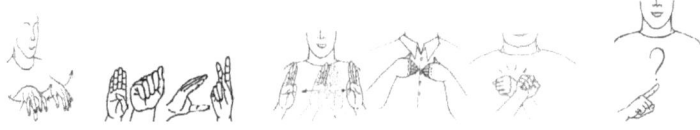

#625.

They've already    turned on the electricity.  The house.  is     ready.

#626.

I       am    worried    about the appearance   of      the floor.

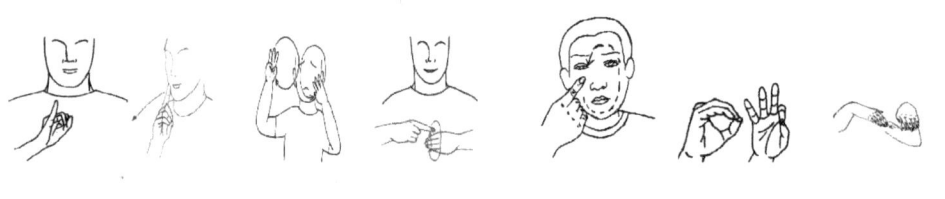

#627.

If     you.  want  a towel,   look   in      that    closet.

#628.

What   style   furniture   do   you   have   ?

#629.

We.   have   drapes   for   the living   room.

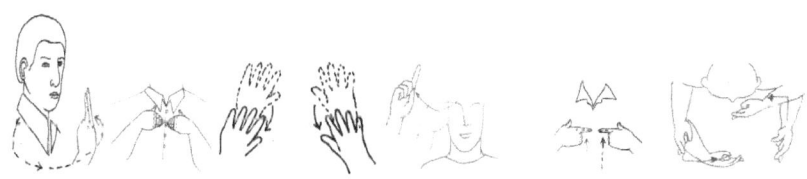

#630.

The house   needs   painting.

#631.

What.   are   you   planning to   wear   today   ?

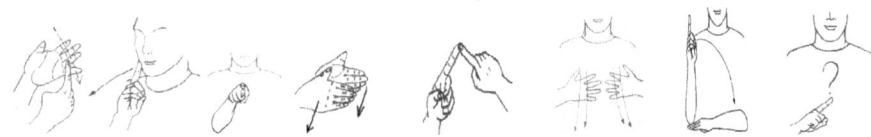

#632.

I    am    planning to    wear    my    blue    suit.

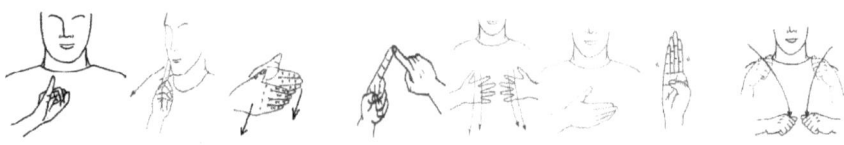

#633.

I    have    two    suits    to    send    to    the cleaners.

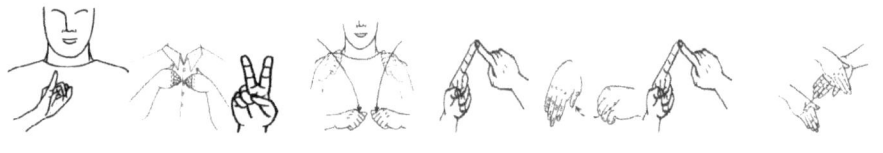

#634.

I    have    some    shirts    to    send    to    the laundry.

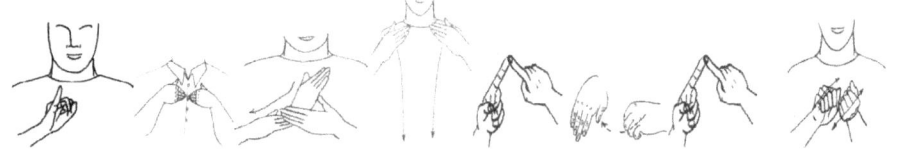

#635.

You    ought    to    have    that    coat    cleaned.

#636.

I've        got        to have    this   shirt  washed.

#637.

All      my      suits      are      dirty.

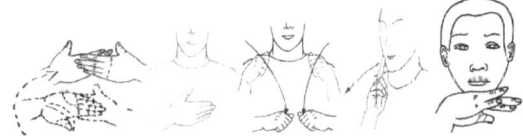

#638.

You'd.    better    wear a light    jacket   it's   chilly    today.

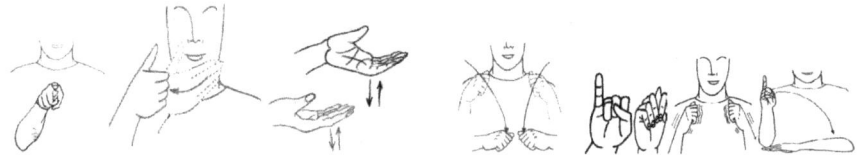

#639.

This    dress    doesn't    fit              me      any      more.

#640.

I     guess     I     have     grown  out

of     these     trousers.

#641.

These     shoes     are     worn-out.

They've     lasted     a long     time.

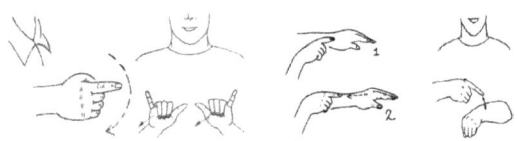

#642.

I     can't     use     this     coat.

#643.

Why        don't  you     get  dressed now   ?

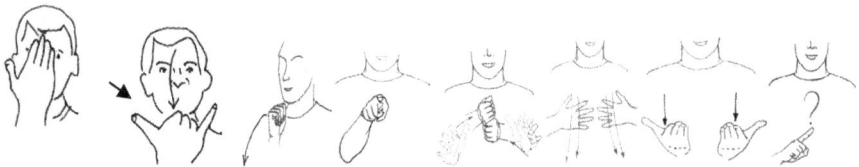

Put on   your   work  clothes.

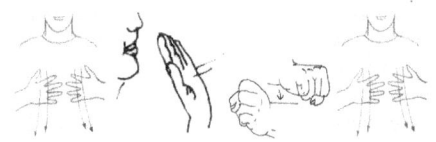

#644.

My.  brother  came   in,    changed   his   clothes,

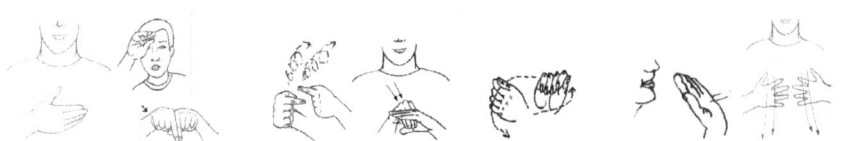

and       went  out.  again.

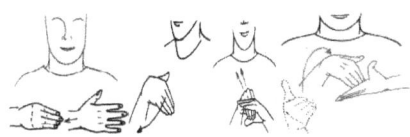

#645.

I   didn't   notice   your      new      hat.

#646.

You     have     your   idea,     and     I     have     mine.

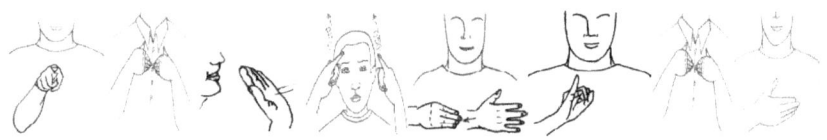

#647.

Your   approach     is  a different   way     than     I   do.

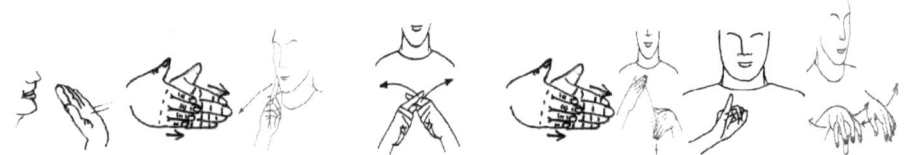

#648.

I    won't    argue  with  you,   but

I    think  you   are   not   fair.

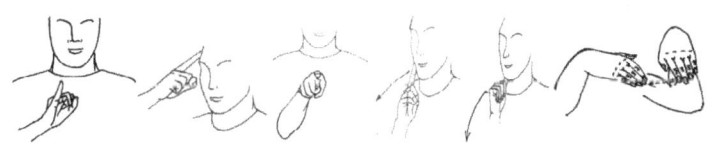

#649.

That    is  an opposite  way      of    thought.

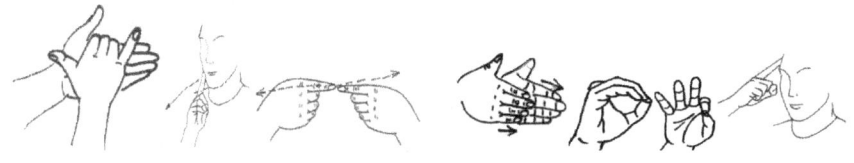

#650.

He   does   have. a lot   of strange   ideas.

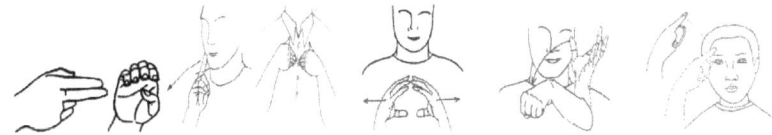

#651.

I    don't  see   any    point  in discussing   further.

#652.

What   other         do       I     have   ?

#653.

Everyone    does have   his own   opinion.

#654.

There are   always     two   sides   to    every thought.

#655.

We    have  opposite  views    on      this.

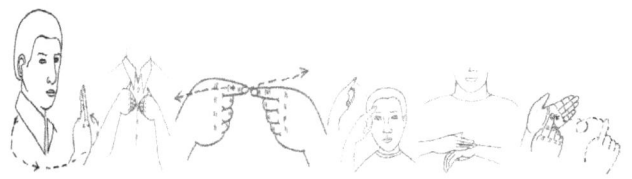

#656.

Please  forgive.  me    I    didn't    mean    to  start an argument.

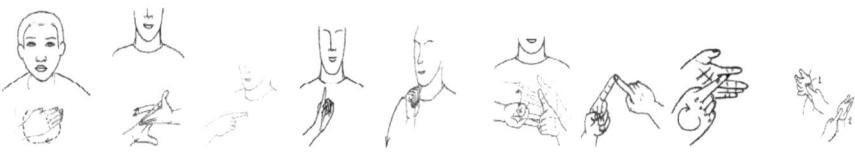

#657.

I    must  know  your  opinion.  Do    you    agree  with    me   ?

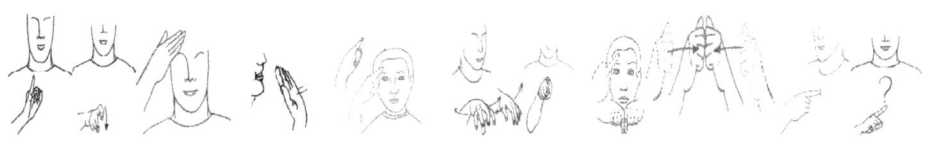

#658.

What      is      your      idea    ?

#659.

Our   ideas   are   not   so far   apart.

#660.

We   can   resolve   our   differences.

#661.

If it   doesn't rain   tomorrow,   I   think   I'll   go   shopping.

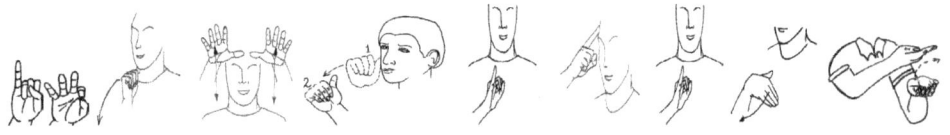

#662.

Maybe   we'll   go,   but   depending   on   the   weather.

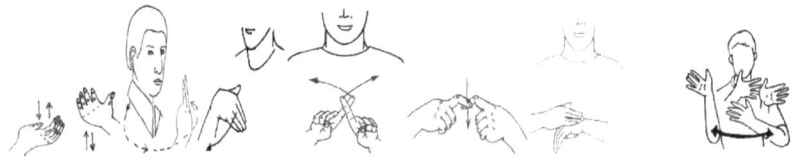

#663.

If    I   have  time  tomorrow, I  think  I'll  get a   haircut.

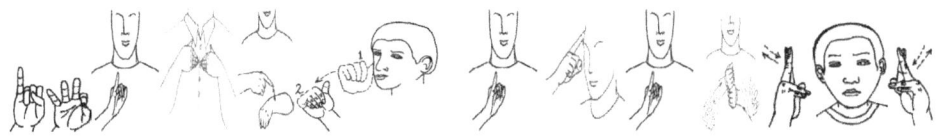

#664.

I   must  remember   to    ask    the barber

not    to   make   my     cut    too    short.

#665.

My   son   wants   to    be  a policeman when he grows up.

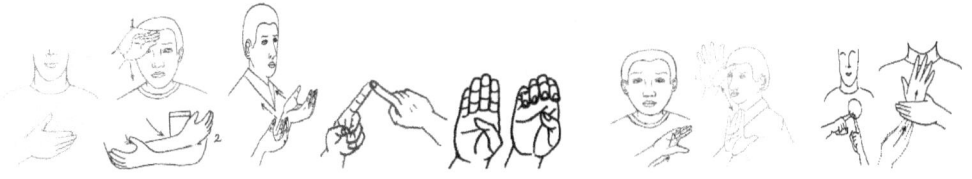

#666.

If    I    finish  my    work ,

I    will      leave     for     New York  Monday

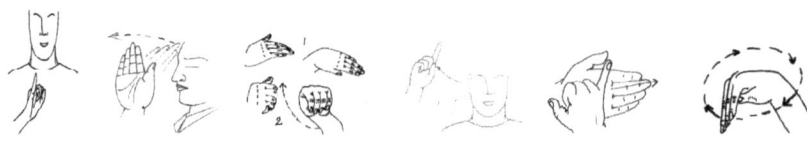

#667.

Suppose  you   couldn't   go   on    the trip,

how   would  you    feel  ?

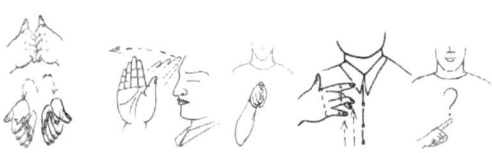

#668.

What would you     say

if     I     say     I couldn't     go     with     you. ?

#669.

If     I     buy     that     Car

I'll     have.     to     borrow     some     money.

#670.

If    I    went    with    you,    I 'd    have    to be

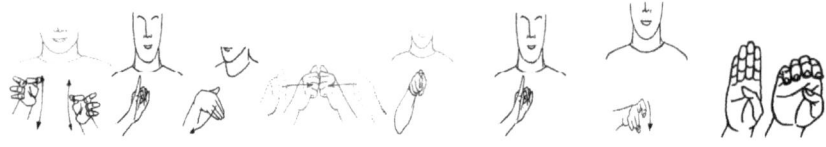

back         by         six o'clock.

#671.

One of these days,    I'd    like        to        take    a vacation.

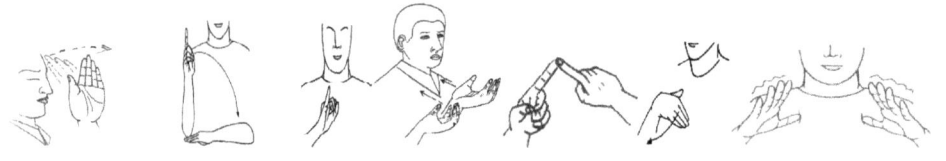

#672.

Soon ,    I    want        to        change    jobs.

#673.

Maybe      he    won't    be able to be   home  for  Christmas.

#674.

We   may be      able   to   help   you.  in some   way.

#675.

If   you   attend the banquet, what would you  wear    ?

#676.

If   you   did not study,   what    would  you have done ?

#677.

I   would have gone   on        the            picnic

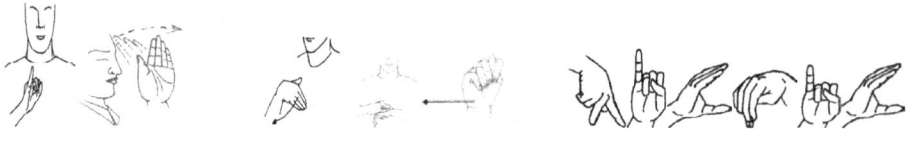

if  it     hadn't   rained.

#678.

If    you     not  sleep, you  would have had time  for  breakfast.

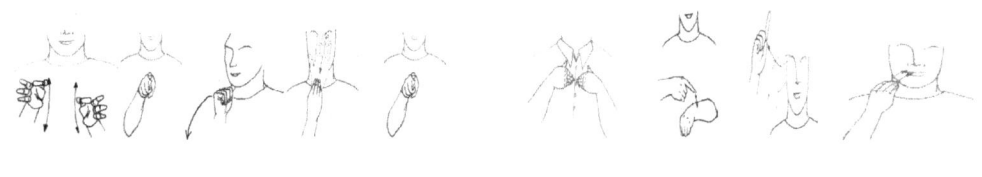

#679.

If    I     had had time,   I    would have    called  you.

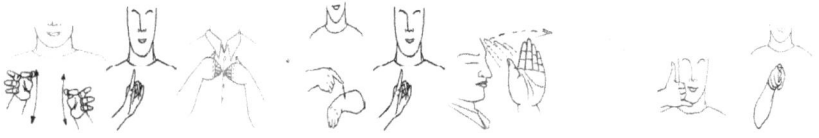

#680.

Would    he    have  seen you  if  you   waved   ?

#681.

If   he      had enough money,

he     would  have.  bought that  house.

#682.

I   wish   `you had called me back the next day

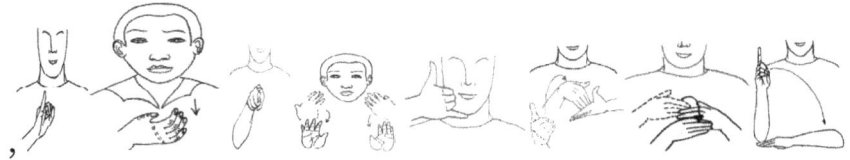

as   I had  asked you.

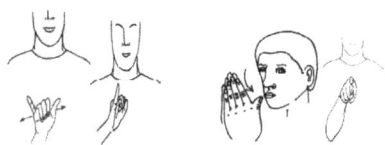

#683.

If    you    hadn't fallen,  you    wouldn't brake

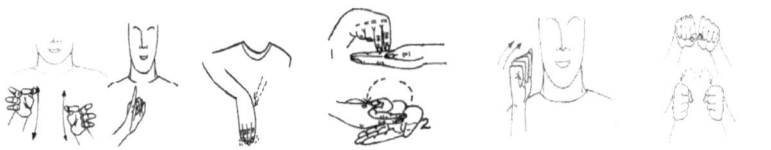

your    leg.

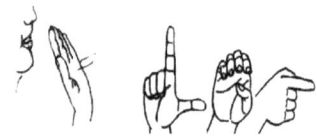

#684.

If    I    knew    you wanted    to    go,

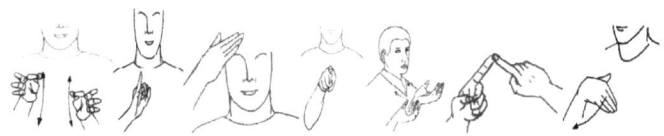

I    would    have    called you.

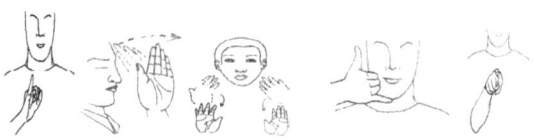

#685.

If    I    known    you    didn't    have    a key,

I      would  not  have   locked the door.

#686.

She      would  have gone  with    me,   but

she      didn't   have   time.

#687.

If    I  had asked for   directions,  I  wouldn't  be lost

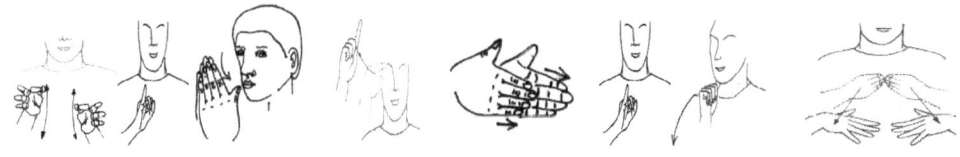

#688.

If   we   could        taken   a vacation,

we     might    not have   wanted     to      go.

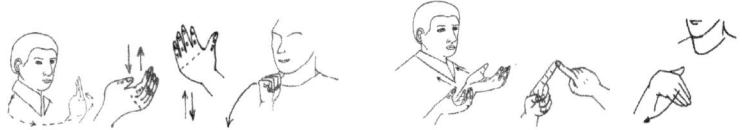

#689. Every thing     would  have been all right   if     you

hadn't   said     that.

#690.

I    wish    we   hadn't  given in so   easily.

#691.

What  is it  you  don't  like  about  winter  weather  ?

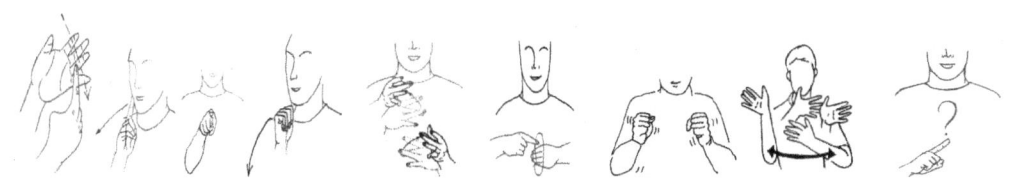

#692.

  I  don't  like it  when the weather becomes  real  cold.

#693.

  I  can't  stand  summer  weather.

#694.

The    thing    I    don't like    about    driving    is

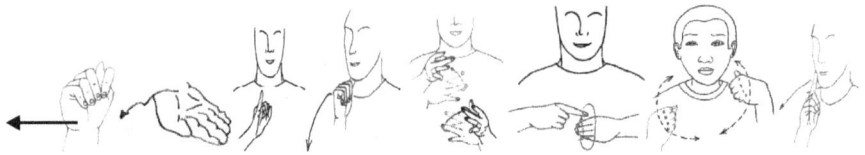

  all the    traffic    on      the    road.

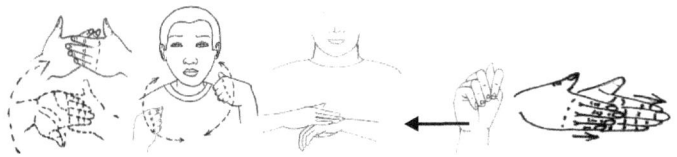

#695.

  He  doesn't  like the   idea    of    going  to bed   early.

696.

  I   like    to   play    baseball.

#697.

I   don't   like                spinach

even though.   I      know.   it's   good   for   me.

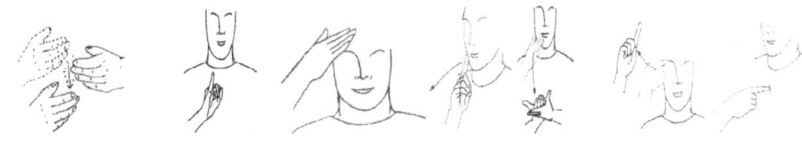

#698.

I        am  afraid you're being  too   particular about   your   food.

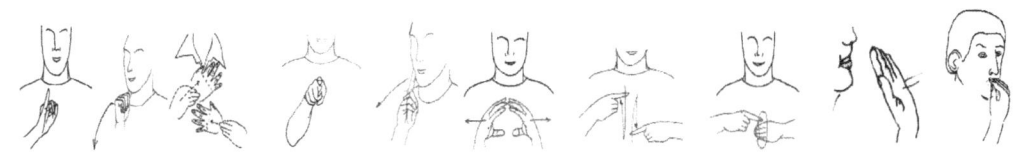

#699.

He        always      finds fault  with    everything.

#700.

She         doesn't   do     anything       I      say.